*What the Experts are Saying About*
# Alcoholism Myths and Realities

"...a wonderful review of the myths of alcoholism, the effects on the brain, its biochemistry and related behavioral outcomes. The focus on destructive behaviors as a symptom and identifier of alcohol and other drug addiction is extraordinarily enlightening."

Jack Buehler, MA, LMHP, LADC, NCAC II

"Doug Thorburn has important insights into the disease which lies behind many of the problems facing families. Divorce, child abuse, spousal abuse, false accusations, parental alienation syndrome—addiction plays a hidden role in these social pathologies far more often than you might imagine."

Glenn Sacks, nationally syndicated radio talk show host

"Doug Thorburn's books are consistently great, and this is his best. If people listen, his work will revolutionize the field of addiction."

Father Jack Shirley, Order of St. Augustine,<br>Author, *Spiritual Reflections for a Recovering Alcoholic*

"An innovative and enlightening examination of alcoholism. *Alcoholism Myths and Realities* explodes the myths that almost everyone believes about addiction."

Joan Harter, M.S., Certified Addictions Treatment Specialist

"WARNING!!! The information contained in this book may burst your bubble—and it could also save your life! Armed with the invaluable knowledge that Doug Thorburn so thoroughly presents, we become empowered to navigate more safely through the minefield of humanity we encounter every day. Read this book! Especially if you DON'T think you are in a relationship—be it intimate, family, friendship, colleague or neighbor—with an addict."

Holly J. Hopkins, Executive Director
I SAW YOU Safety & Scholarship Foundation, Inc.

"As an interventionist, I have seen countless families affected by a loved one's alcoholism. *Alcoholism Myths and Realities* gives them the tools to identify this disease and intervene without guilt."

Pat Moomey, Certified Addictions Treatment Specialist

"A sensitive, easy-to-comprehend work and a crowning achievement!"

Irwin Zucker, President, Promotion in Motion
Founder/Pres. Emeritus, Book Publicists of Southern California

"One of the most important messages that anyone could deliver to society. I don't understand why people are deaf to this and have been for centuries."

Robert Prechter, CMT, Author, *Socionomics*

"Brilliant insights. A must read—not just for those who know they are involved with alcoholics, but even more so for everyone else."

Bob Wall, Martial Artist, Actor

# Alcoholism
## Myths and Realities

# Alcoholism
## Myths and Realities

### Removing the Stigma
### of Society's Most
### Destructive Disease

## By Doug Thorburn

Copyright © 2005 Doug Thorburn

PUBLISHED BY GALT PUBLISHING
P. O. Box 7777
Northridge, CA 91327-7777


Address the author c/o Galt Publishing
or at DougThorburn@PrevenTragedy.com


Cover design by Dreu Pennington-McNeil
Cover photograph © Liquid/Nonstock

ISBN: 0-9675788-2-5

LCCN: 2004116249

Printed in the United States
0 9 8 7 6 5 4 3 2 1
First Edition

## Disclaimer

The purpose of this book is to educate laypersons and healthcare professionals about alcoholism. Please do not consider the information given in this
book to be the equivalent of treatment or an individual consultation. The person dealing with possible alcoholics is strongly advised to seek the help of
chemical dependency experts, as well as attend Alcoholics Anonymous <u>and</u>
Al-Anon meetings. This book is sold with the understanding that the author
and publisher shall have neither liability nor responsibility to any person or
entity with respect to any injury or damage caused or alleged to have been
caused, directly or indirectly, by the information in this book.

# Contents

# Acknowledgments

I wish to thank the addiction experts on whose shoulders I have stood, particularly James Graham, Katherine Ketcham, James Milam and Vernon Johnson. In addition, Jennifer Huddleston deserves special mention as my sounding board and much-needed critic, along with Scott Dorfman who has previously offered brilliant input on communicating simply. My dear friends Mel Kreger and Joseph Sullivan have provided valuable support throughout. The officers and board members of the PrevenTragedy Foundation, Pat Moomey, Patricia Morrow, Patricia Oliver Ferguson, Joan Harter, Mike Kennedy, Joe Pilkington, Robert Richards and friend of the Foundation, Laura Sisk, also provided moral and intellectual support. Most important, I give my love and thanks to my favorite skeptic, my wife Marty, for putting up with long hours of research and writing, as well as challenging me on several key assumptions without which this book would not have been possible.

# Introduction

This book is intended to expose the myths about alcoholism that permeate our society's thinking. Most believe that we give the benefit of the doubt by suggesting explanations other than alcoholism as the root of misbehaviors. Instead, we need to assume the opposite and look for alcoholism first. Rather than thinking we are helping by providing a safety net, we need to understand that pain is by far the most effective motivator in guiding the alcoholic into treatment. By discrediting the myths that surround this disease, the stigma that instills emotion in the identification of alcoholism can be eliminated. Only then can those affected, whether family, friends, co-workers or society, offer tough love with a clear conscience.

Alcoholism* is the most misunderstood of all diseases. This is rather surprising, since one out of ten people has this disease and we are all directly or indirectly affected. Yet the doctors and psychologists whom we trust to treat diseases and mental disorders are almost completely untrained in understanding and diagnosing the affliction. Medical doctors take as few as 24 classroom hours on the subject, virtually all on treating withdrawal and none on diagnosis. Psychologists are schooled in the idea that childhood trauma and other negative environmental factors can cause alcoholism, even though the evidence shows that such influences only shape its course.

Secondary diseases are usually diagnosed long before alcoholism is identified, even though the latter is the root cause or primary contributing factor to at least 300 other illnesses and

*Alcoholism is used throughout this book as an abbreviation for the more accurate "alcohol and other drug addiction" and includes addiction to any drug capable of causing distortions of perception and memory. The term is defined in Myth #96.

disorders. Emergency room medical personnel treat symptoms of addiction, including accidents, in an estimated 50 to 80% of admissions, yet rarely test for alcohol or other drugs in the system. The schools implore adolescents to "just say no to drugs!" focusing on the drug rather than the person on it, a primary problem for only 10% of users. The media misinform by failing to connect the dots between bad behaviors and alcoholism; the movies do so by making the portrayal of alcoholism obvious only in its latter stages, or when illegal drugs are involved. Most people balk at calling someone of like politics or personality "an alcoholic," even if some of their behaviors are bizarre or destructive. Yet, many wouldn't hesitate to suggest that a person with whom they differ who drinks the equivalent of a bottle of wine every day "must be an alcoholic." Aspects essential to the identification of alcoholism, including the time frame over which the drinking occurred, the drinker's weight and change in behaviors, are rarely considered.

This gross unawareness results from the stigma, which makes others reluctant to diagnose or even suggest the possibility of alcoholism. Epilepsy, diabetes, leprosy, tuberculosis and other diseases were attributed in past centuries to character defects such as lack of morals or witchcraft until their true causes were identified.[1] Over one hundred years after the stigma of the last of these diseases was largely removed, those labeled as alcoholics continue to suffer disgrace. This is evident in society's attitude toward alcoholism. Almost all with addicted family members in rehab are ashamed. One who is called "an alcoholic" can bring a lawsuit for defamation of character, as if alcoholism makes the person inherently evil. If someone engages in bad behavior, most think the benefit of the doubt is given by suggesting anything other than alcoholism. In other words, it's better to think the cause of misbehaviors is that the person is fundamentally flawed, has incredibly poor judgment, or suffers from mental illness, than to label him "alcoholic."

Even chemical dependency experts, who have been trained to understand the disease, along with recovering alcoholics who have lived it, help perpetuate this stigma. As we will see later, using a flawed definition, the words and phrases employed to describe alcoholism evoke false impressions. Alcoholism is said to require loss of control over use, which makes it sound more like a character flaw than a disease. Yet, loss of control is but a latter-stage symptom, generally not occurring until decades after its inception. Terms such as "denial" and "abuse" convey a grossly distorted view of alcoholics and their perceptions, while phrases such as "he can't control his drinking" and "he's a problem drinker" serve to mislead alcoholics and non-alcoholics alike. As a result, those in early recovery often experience extraordinary shame, which can lead to severe depression, relapse and suicide.

Experts rarely stress the need to impose consequences for misbehaviors. As a result, society ends up protecting addicts from consequences without having any idea that doing so only extends the period of active addiction and, therefore, misery for everyone exposed. While lip service is given to the idea of privately imposing consequences, family and friends rarely assist alcoholics in experiencing proper repercussions for inappropriate behavior. Experts and recovering alcoholics alike hardly ever emphasize that the imposition of responsibility is a vital part of what, for many, is essentially a "cure" for alcoholism: keeping a promise to never use again. Recovering addicts almost uniformly fail to thank those who initiated part of that cure, leaving the rest of us wondering whether we can truly help by being so harsh. Uncompromising tough love is usually offered only when there are no other options. Because so much of what occurred while drinking is buried in the subconscious or, simply, not remembered, recovering alcoholics rarely explain that extreme actions on the part of close persons were necessary to get them sober.

The biochemistry of alcoholism has never been adequately and simply described. Early-stage alcoholism is rarely, if ever, identified, while the media report on adolescent-like, bizarre or destructive behaviors of celebrities, politicians and others without suggesting that the impetus behind such conduct is almost always this disease. By debunking the myths, we can eliminate the stigma that allows the typical addict to engage in dozens or even hundreds of incidents adversely affecting the lives of others, while the cause goes unrecognized. Only then will we have a chance at identifying the addict before the oftentimes decades-long creep toward latter-stage alcoholism causes the body to give out. Intervention and recovery is possible only with such identification; yet, the addict is incapable of self-diagnosis. The rest of us need to stop being afraid of making the call.

"Some people believe that the label 'alcoholic' transforms a person into an outcast akin to a leper. But, if leprosy is a disease, should a doctor who has proof that a person has leprosy keep that fact a secret lest he label the person a leper? Is not the real challenge for the doctor to continue making the diagnosis to change society's views toward leprosy?"
   —George E. Vaillant[2]

# 1

# Alcoholism Made Simple: the Brain, the Biological Process & Inheritance

### Myth #1
### "Brain damage occurs only in obvious alcoholics."

There is no difference in aggregate levels of misbehaviors and personality problems in children raised in non-alcoholic homes, whether or not they develop alcoholism as adults.[3] Practicing alcoholics engage in erratically destructive behaviors, while non-alcoholics rarely do. In recovery, alcoholics generally become, over time, gentle, kind, honest and non-destructive. These long-term observations of the life cycle of typical alcoholics suggest there is something very different about their brains while actively drinking vs. when not, whether before or after the drinking career. Since poor behaviors usually begin at or near the time of the first drinking episode, alcohol must be changing the brain's biochemistry. And, it must be occurring long before he or she becomes an obvious alcoholic, in which the personal and professional life has fallen apart.

To understand this, the biochemistry of alcoholism must be described. Don't let this scare you; it's really quite simple. Once understood, almost everything that seemed crazy and implausible about human behavior, whether public or private begins to make sense.

The human body converts alcohol first into a poison, acetaldehyde, and then into acetate, both of which find their way to the brain. While the former substance — in the same class of chemicals as formaldehyde — perversely makes the drinker feel good, the latter causes feelings of nausea, hangover and sleepiness. Now think about it: if a person experiences a quick conversion into acetate, he feels lousy or sleepy and is unlikely to keep drinking. If, on the other hand, the body blocks the conversion of acetaldehyde into acetate, the former works its magic and he feels good. It shouldn't be surprising if this person, experiencing a buildup of the former substance and little or no increase in the latter, continues to drink. *Therefore, the speed at which the body converts alcohol into acetate determines a person's predisposition to alcoholism.*

It's that simple.

The non-alcoholic's liver slowly turns alcohol into acetaldehyde, then quickly into acetate. As a result, there is little or no buildup of poison in the brain and instead quick feedback from the acetate-induced ill feeling, which serves to stop the drinking. This generally occurs at relatively low blood alcohol levels, usually .04 to .10 per cent. The top range is barely legally drunk for purposes of operating a motor vehicle.

On the other hand, the alcoholic liver converts alcohol into acetaldehyde *quickly* and then into acetate *slowly*. There is no immediate feedback (nausea, etc.) suggesting that the drinker slow down. Instead, the buildup of acetaldehyde causes a release of "feel-good" neurotransmitters called isoquinolines, which are opiate-like substances. The "I'm feeling fine" response serves as positive feedback to keep on drinking. The top range of blood alcohol level-BAL-to which most non-alcoholics ever drink is where the typical addict is barely getting started. If it stopped there all would be well; after all, there's nothing wrong with feeling really good. However, for alcoholics, this is where the problems begin.

Unfortunately, acetaldehyde, the poison, causes brain damage. Evidence that this occurs even during the hidden early stages (usually the first drinking occasions) is generally observable almost immediately in behaviors. Most parents chalk this up to adolescence. However, the changes should be assumed alcohol or other drug-related unless proven otherwise. Eventually, as poor behaviors continue and actual evidence of addictive use is uncovered, we can attribute the transformation to alcoholism.

When no other drugs are used, obvious personality changes may not become apparent without observing behaviors during and after several drinking events. Few alcoholics act badly every time they drink. On the other hand, they will misbehave at least some of the time. One set of misbehaviors occurs when young people become licensed to drive. Alcoholic teenagers will almost always, often with regularity, drive while intoxicated (we'll later discover why alcoholics can be *expected* to engage in such behaviors). This impaired judgment, manifest in behaviors, is indicative of brain damage rooted in alcoholism, even in the hidden early stage.

## Myth #2
## "The average age at which one becomes an alcoholic is 40."

Or 30, or 50. Any age but the early teens. Yet, most recovering alcoholics tell us they triggered alcoholism during their first drinking episode, usually at age 12 or 13. Looking back, they realize that alcohol did something different for them than for others. They often say, "I felt powerful." The feeling is described in almost heavenly terms as a "glow" or a "lift." We'll discover later that addicts act like they think they are Gods. If they act this way, they must think this, even if only on a subconscious level. If you felt god-like, you'd feel glowing and powerful too.

The buildup of poison on the brain results in brain damage causing distortions of perception and memory. The key distortion leads the afflicted person to believe that everything he says or does during a drinking event (and eventually, in many cases, in-between) is good or right and nothing bad or wrong.

This opinion of his own perfection is the reason he develops a god-like sense of self, which translates into an inordinately large sense of self-importance, or an "inflated ego."

While we can't read his mind, we can see the resulting misbehaviors, which may become extraordinarily gruesome. Sometimes, these are observable at or near the inception of alcoholism, often during adolescence. For example, the behaviors of Eric Harris became deadly at a very young age, as did those of Jeffrey Dahmer and Ted Bundy. Harris, whose favorite drink at age 18 was whiskey, had been taking Luvox, prescribed for Obsessive-Compulsive Personality Disorders and frequently used in treating depression, when he and Dylan Klebold murdered 13 innocents at Columbine High School in 1999. Dahmer and Bundy were obvious teenage alcoholics and became serial murderers in their late teens and twenties. Seemingly mild-mannered Charles Andrew Williams, who at 15 inflicted mayhem at a high school near San Diego, California in early 2001, killing two and wounding 13, had a history of drug use.[4] As a young teen, he is said to have shared a pastime with the tougher boys in the neighborhood: smoking marijuana and stealing vodka and tequila from a local grocery store.[5]

However, the behaviors of most alcoholics are often not so grisly or even overtly destructive. One of the most common misbehaviors exhibited by early-stage alcoholics is promiscuity. This is a more subtle, less obvious way by which to wield power over sexual partners, which can be destructive even if masked with charm. It is this perverse need to misuse power, especially capriciously, which leads to many of the bad behaviors that observers frequently witness in early-stage alcoholics.

# Myth #3
## "Alcoholism is a spiritual disease."

Recovering alcoholics often confuse cause and effect, believing that loss of spirituality precipitated their alcoholism.

The biochemistry of alcoholism results in an inflated ego. Having an inordinately large sense of self-importance interferes with spirituality. If you are God, there can be no other God. As recovering alcoholics often say, in active addiction they were the center of their universe, and yours.

An effect of alcoholism (and, therefore, a clue to its existence) is loss of spirituality. Recovery requires abstinence and ego deflation. Without both, good solid recovery in which behaviors markedly improve is impossible. The 12-Step Program works to deflate the ego by replacing it with a higher power. Since loss of spirit is only an effect of alcoholism, it cannot be its cause. Regaining spirituality is, however, imperative for recovery.

# Myth #4
## "You can choose not to be an alcoholic."

You can no more choose to not have alcoholism than to have or not have early-onset diabetes. All the alcoholic can do is choose not to drink. However, due to the biochemistry that makes him feel good and, at the same time, causes distortions in perception and memory, he cannot see that his drinking is a problem. Therefore, he needs to be convinced to make this decision.

It's a difficult choice. After all, alcohol (and, usually, numerous other drugs) not only makes the early-stage alcoholic feel good, but also powerful. His brain chemistry distorts perceptions and memory so that he views everything from the perspective that he is always right. Ask yourself this question: would you want to stop using a chemical that, at some level, made you not only feel great, but also god-like? Why would *you* abstain?

You wouldn't. This is the reason we need to help the addict make that choice by connecting his use of the drug to pain resulting from logical consequences. As long as close persons protect him from such outcomes, the odds of making the correct decision are remote. Instead, everyone must do all they can to hold the addict accountable for misbehaviors, which includes total disengagement from personal and professional relationships for as long as active addiction continues.

The difficulty in disengaging is not only that every close person needs to learn the trademark behaviors of practicing alcoholics, but also that disenabling must follow. Even one enabler can greatly reduce the odds of permanent sobriety. While this may be challenging, it is not insurmountable. It will become easier once the stigma surrounding alcoholism is removed, allowing family, friends and associates to freely discuss the possibility that alcoholism accounts for misbehaviors.

# Myth #5
## "The addict is in denial."

The damage that the poison, acetaldehyde, inflicts on the brain results in distortions of perception. The key distortion experienced by the alcoholic, coined "euphoric recall" by the late alcoholism authority Vernon Johnson, causes the addict to remember everything he does or says in a self-favoring light.[6] He does not act badly; you do. He commits no wrongs; you do. If he does something for which he should be held accountable, it is because *you* made him commit the act. Hence, euphoric recall leads to what appear to be rationalizations. However, he truly believes that no matter how grotesque, what he did was the right thing to do under the circumstances.

Or, he may remember nothing. Many recovering addicts admit to having no idea how they got home (or wherever they "came to") after a day (or two, or three) of bingeing. Their first thought is often to check the car's front fender for bloodstains. These episodes, termed "blackouts," are periods of time during which events do not even enter the memory banks and, therefore, *cannot* be recalled.

He may also remember nothing at the time, having unintentionally engaged in "memory repression." While we are all capable of repressing memories, the addict does so far more completely and efficiently. There may be a good reason for this: if he could remember everything he did while in active addiction during a moment of clarity, he might go into irreversible emotional shock and become suicidal. His brain is merely doing what it can and must to prevent self-destruction.

"Denial" implies a willful refusal to not admit to something. Since alcoholism causes self-favoring distortions of perception and, often, no memory at all, there is nothing to admit. One cannot be in denial about something that he is incapable of seeing.

The term is an extremely misleading descriptor, responsible for tremendous misconceptions about alcoholism, which results in much of its stigma. A person in "denial" should know better; therefore, the alcoholic is unintelligent. Worse, a willful attempt to not admit to something makes the person a liar. However, the truth of the matter is, he usually is not stupid and the disease compels him to make what appear to be lies. He is, then, not in denial; he cannot be.

# Myth #6
# "With a Blood Alcohol Level between .10 and .24 per cent, even an alcoholic would appear inebriated."

Teetotalers begin to show the classic signs of drunkenness, including staggered gait and slurred speech, at BALs as low as .05 per cent. Normal drinkers (i.e., non-alcoholics) display such signs at BALs typically no higher than .10 per cent. However, early- to middle-stage alcoholics often appear stone cold sober at BALs of .20 per cent and even up to .24 per cent (three times the federal legal limit for operating a motor vehicle).

Hundreds of millions saw Henri Paul in the hotel video just prior to the reckless stunt in which he and Princess Diana were killed. Not only did he not look drunk in the video; bodyguard Trevor Rees-Jones, who was up close and personal, said that Henri Paul "did not appear to have [even] been drinking." Yet his BAL was .178 per cent, the equivalent of almost two bottles of wine or twelve shots of 80-proof liquor in four hours for a 200-pound person. Most non-alcoholics would be doing a face-plant after consuming this much booze. Not only was Paul apparently alert, but he also didn't make a fatal mistake in a 35 mile-per hour zone in a tunnel with giant pillars until he hit 90 mph. No one would likely have been the wiser if he had stayed below 80 mph.

Drug Recognition Experts are law enforcers who undergo special training in non-intrusive methods of determining which class or classes of drug or drugs a suspect is under the influence. These experts report that alcoholics have passed standard balance and coordination tests (which include walking a straight line, bringing the finger to the nose from outstretched arm with eyes closed and standing on one leg) only to undergo blood tests measuring BALs as high as .28 per cent and beyond.

The author has asked numerous bartenders whether they could identify a highly tolerant early-stage alcoholic walking into a bar with a BAL of .15 per cent. This is the only group other than chemical dependency experts that almost uniformly gives the right answer. However, even this elite group usually believes the next myth.

## Myth #7
## "Two or three drinks per hour are needed to maintain a given Blood Alcohol Level."

When bartenders are asked the number of drinks required hourly for maintenance (to hold steady at a given BAL), the response is, typically, two or three. While this group of alcohol specialists isn't even close, no other class of people does any better.

The human body processes alcohol at roughly .015 per cent per hour, regardless of weight, sex or other factors. Each standard "drink" (12 ounces of beer with 5% alcohol, 5 ounces of wine containing 12% alcohol or 1.5 ounces of 80-proof liquor-equivalent to 40% alcohol) increases the BAL by a relatively fixed amount depending on the person's weight. One drink increases a 200-pounder's BAL by .02 per cent and three-quar-

14

ters of a drink by .015 per cent. Since the liver processes alcohol at .015 per cent per hour, only three-quarters of a drink per hour is needed for a 200-pound person to maintain the BAL (the point at which assimilation equals intake). Not even a bartender would have a clue that a patron with a BAL of .18 per cent, sipping his drink at the rate of 3.5 ounces of wine, 9 ounces of beer or barely over one ounce of hard liquor *per hour*, is a person with early-stage alcoholism.

He'd have even less of a clue observing a 120-pound person sipping a glass of wine. While she also processes the drug at .015 per cent per hour, each drink increases her BAL by .03 per cent and each half drink, .015 per cent. Therefore, half of a drink, or 2.5 ounces of wine, 6 ounces of beer or .75 ounce of 80-proof liquor — per hour — is all that's required for maintenance. So, she could walk into a bar, your home, work, or a restaurant for brunch late one Sunday morning with a BAL of .18 per cent and sip her Cabernet, Merlot, Chardonnay or champagne, without anyone being the wiser. Unless, of course, we begin to notice the bizarre or destructive conduct in which she will engage from time to time *and* understand that alcoholism is usually the impetus behind such behaviors.

| Weight | Drinks needed per hour to maintain the BAL, once at a desired level | Drinks needed per hour to increase BAL by .03 per cent |
|---|---|---|
| 120 pounds | 0.5 | 1.5 |
| 200 pounds | 0.75 | 2.25 |

Drinks needed over four hours to reach a BAL of:

| | Beer | Wine | 80-proof liquor |
|---|---|---|---|
| One drink equals: | 12 oz. | 5 oz. | 1.5 oz. |

| Weight | 0.08 per cent | 0.10 per cent | 0.15 per cent | 0.18 per cent | 0.24 per cent |
|---|---|---|---|---|---|
| 120 pound | 4.67 | 5.33 | 7 | 8 | 10 |
| 200 pound | 7 | 8 | 10.5 | 12 | 15 |

Having no idea how little alcohol is required to maintain a given BAL was one of the keys to my inability to detect alcoholism in a person with whom I was once romantically involved. It was also a case in which a little bit of knowledge proved to be dangerous. I knew to look for gulping as a clue to alcoholism. She didn't gulp. I never saw the vodka mixed with her milk or the Bailey's added to her coffee, before we nursed a bottle of wine over an evening.

# Myth #8
# "Three drinks will make
# anyone legally intoxicated."

As we have seen, each drink increases the blood alcohol level by a given amount determined mostly by the weight of the drinker, while time serves to slowly offset this. If alcohol is processed as quickly as it is drunk, the BAL cannot increase. Three drinks spread evenly over six hours will not make any-one drunk; in fact, the BAL will remain at barely over zero for anyone over 120 pounds. Three drinks increase the BAL of a 120-pound person to .09 per cent if drunk instantly; over two hours, .03 per cent is processed, bringing the BAL to .06 per cent. A non-alcoholic may appear a little tipsy at this level. Since a person weighing 200 pounds experiences an increase in BAL of .02 per cent per drink, she'll test at .06 per cent if she has three drinks in a very short period. By spreading this amount over two hours, her BAL won't exceed .03 per cent, a level at which very few appear drunk.

Even at double a BAL of .09 per cent, demonstrated in the classic example of Henri Paul (whose body fluid tests reported a BAL of nearly .18 per cent), early- to middle-stage alcoholics won't seem "drunk." The non-alcoholic likely looks—and acts—tipsy at half Paul's level, but she is not our concern. Usually a "happy" drunk, she often conks out at about this point. The response to this myth, then, depends upon the weight of the drinker, the time period over which the drinking occurs and whether or not she has alcoholism. A person not having this disease may appear inebriated with a BAL at which an alcoholic is barely getting started. The latter may not show the classic signs of inebriation until she reaches a BAL as high as .24 per cent, even if her behaviors give away the secret long before.

## Myth #9 (a "half-truth")
## "He has a hangover because he drank too much last night."

While this may be true, the inference is often that if he has a hangover, there must be alcoholism. This may suggest the opposite: if there is no hangover, there cannot be alcoholism. Both conclusions are incorrect.

Non-alcoholics almost always get hangovers when they drink too much, which isn't a whole lot compared to those having alcoholism. They may suffer with BALs as low as .04 per cent, not quite two drinks in an hour for a 120-pound person and less than three for a person weighing 200 pounds. They may even begin to feel queasy during the drinking episode, which provides quick feedback to discontinue drinking. Usually, the cue is taken seriously.

Most with alcoholism do not experience anything like a hangover while imbibing, even at extremely high BALs. Instead, any ill feeling occurs far removed from the drinking. Therefore, the hangover is linked with *not* drinking. The fact that the alcoholic feels great while using and not so good between drinking episodes increases the odds that he will quickly return to drinking.

Many alcoholics never have hangovers. Researchers found that 50% of the subjects in a study of alcoholics "reported no hangovers within the past year or more and 23% reported that they had never experienced a hangover, despite very heavy drinking."[7] Senator Joseph McCarthy is said to have been one of these. A biographer, Richard Rovere, describes McCarthy often drinking a fifth between midnight and 5am. He'd then "catch a couple of hours sleep, and be at his office at eight or nine," ready to begin another day of making false accusations,[8] a serious misbehavior for which alcoholics are known.

## Myth #10
## "Light-to-moderate users of alcohol account for most of the lost-work days because they make up most of the work force."

Research was recently released showing that light-to-moderate drinkers cause most problems in the workplace, usually a result of hangovers. Light-to-moderate was defined as zero to three drinks per day for men and zero to one for women.[9]

As mentioned, three drinks in quick succession results in a BAL of .06 per cent for a 200-pound person. One drink will raise the BAL to .03 per cent in a 120-pounder. This level of drinking cannot cause hangovers. If it did, a non-alcoholic with responsibilities would simply stop drinking. Therefore, the purported findings are impossible to confirm based on anything remotely resembling real-life experience. The researchers stated, "Although light-to-moderate drinkers account for fewer absent days per drinker, they represent the overwhelming majority of alcohol consumers. Because there are many more light-to-moderate drinkers than chronic alcoholics, their contribution to the total lost productivity due to alcohol is substantially larger."[10] They made the amazing assumption that because there are more social drinkers, they must have more hangovers, the costs of which must be greater than that of alcoholic drinkers.

The underlying assumption seems to be that non-alcoholics have the same number of hangovers as alcoholics. These researchers could easily conclude that non-alcoholics, comprising 90% of the population, must commit 90% of DUI offenses, or that alcoholics, consisting of 10% of the population, must comprise only 10% of incarcerated prisoners. Faulty research and illogical conclusions such as this not only help perpetuate many of the myths creating the stigma from which alcoholism suffers, but also spread tremendous misconceptions about alcohol.

## Myth #11
## "Drugs are inherently addictive; every user is a potential addict."

The bogeyman of drugs, heroin, is considered by many to be the most addictive of all. Yet, not even this drug is as easy to become addicted to as most seem to think.

The human body converts heroin into morphine in about two minutes. Yet 90% of those given the latter when hospitalized walk out, none the worse, not craving morphine, heroin, Oxycontin, Vicodin, Tylenol with codeine or any other drug. About 10% will crave these drugs and do anything to get them. These are the addicts, any of whom could become addicted to heroin if only it was available. Conversely, every heroin addict tells us that in a pinch he would take codeine as a substitute. And many such addicts tell us they triggered this addiction with codeine or one of the other opiate-like drugs. Most were already alcoholics.

The reason heroin and other illegal drugs seem so addictive is that typically, only addicts use them. However, Viet Nam, where many soldiers shot up heroin, was not typical. Of these, 95% returned to the States and stopped their use cold turkey. Either they were not addicts or they were alcoholics content with alcohol or other legal or easy-to-obtain substitutes. Back in the United States, only the predisposed continued to use the socially unacceptable and prohibited heroin.

The idea that heroin is, in itself, extremely addictive flies in the face of the fact that it usually takes months of use to become physically addicted. A typical addict may snort for several months, skin pop for several more and then begin mainlining, taking another two or so months before a break in use results in physical withdrawal.[11]

The problem, therefore, isn't the drug. Like opiates in its

many forms, most of us can drink alcohol with impunity and not act destructively. Some use marijuana non-addictively and even cocaine, although regular users of illegal drugs, since they run the risk of heavy punishment if caught, can be presumed to be addicts. Only one of seven drinkers in the United States drinks alcoholically. Most people don't have a problem saying no to such drugs, simply because they are not addicts.

Further evidence that the drug is not the issue can be extrapolated from the fact that those using prescriptions in non-pharmaceutically prescribed doses are addicts just like any other. As Newsweek put it when reporting on Rush Limbaugh's having been outed for pharmaceutical drug addiction, "it's extremely rare for a person with no history of substance abuse to become addicted to Oxy-Contin after using it correctly."[12] Limbaugh, should he remain clean for at least a few years, will eventually attest to the fact that his was simply a rich-man's version of a heroin addict.

In addition, the rate of addiction to currently illegal drugs seems to be stable over time, including eras during which the drugs were legal. The percentage of the population estimated to be addicted to cocaine has remained at roughly 1.3% over extended periods: in 1914 when the drug was sold in grocery stores, in 1979, a few years before the drug war began in earnest, as well as in 2000, after years of futile attempts at eradicating the drug.[13] Experimentation with drugs would likely increase under decriminalization. However, casual or occasional use by non-addicts, with whom we need not be concerned, should not be confused with addictive use, which is where the focus of family, friends, co-workers and law enforcement should be.

## Myth #12
### "But she's only on Xanax. This shouldn't be a problem; after all, it's only available by prescription."

Xanax is a benzodiazepine, just like Valium (diazepam). A central nervous system (CNS) depressant, this is in a class of sedative-hypnotics that also includes Miltown (one of alcoholic-actress Bette Davis' favorite drugs), Equinil, Halcion, Restoril, Ativan, chloral hydrate, Placydil, Klonopin, clonazepam and any other drug ending in "pam." If the person has alcoholism, this myth is the equivalent of saying "but she's only on alcohol."

Noelle Bush, daughter of Governor Jeb Bush of Florida, was charged with prescription fraud "after she tried to obtain the anti-anxiety drug Xanax from a pharmacy."[14] In commenting on the case, Terrance Woodworth, deputy director of the Office of Diversion Control for the Drug Enforcement Administration, said that drugs such as Xanax have "long been the most prescribed and available and abused of the controlled substances. It's an amazing amount of abuse, and it's all ages.'" Xanax is more addictive (for those who are predisposed to addiction) than are other benzodiazepines.[15]

Just because a doctor prescribes a drug does not mean that the patient isn't an addict. Few physicians understand addiction. They generally aren't trained in the field, many are addicts themselves (recovering alcoholic M.D.s estimate that upwards of 20% of doctors are afflicted with the disease) and they frequently misdiagnose. Many recovering addicts tell us doctors were their biggest enablers, prescribing drugs that potentiated others, including alcohol. It takes very little Xanax or any other CNS depressant with a seemingly innocuous amount of alcohol to create a good high for an addict.

Nor do doctors know to ask patients whether they are in recovery before prescribing drugs. Rush Limbaugh may have been victim to this: as the Newsweek article implied, he was probably a recovering alcoholic when he first asked his doctor for a remedy to alleviate his back pain. The M.D. probably didn't know to ask, or wouldn't have guessed that someone of Limbaugh's stature and functionality could be an addict. On the other hand he may have asked, in which case Limbaugh may not yet have known to identify himself as a recovering alcoholic, since perhaps he only "gave up drinking" some years before.

# Chart of Psychoactive Drugs*

| | Stimulants | CNS Depressants | Narcotics |
|---|---|---|---|
| Legal | alcohol**<br>caffeine | alcohol** | alcohol** |
| Legal by Prescription | Adderal<br>amphetamines<br>Benzedrine<br>Dexedrine<br>Dextrostat<br>Ritalin | barbiturates:<br>Fiorinal<br>Fioricet<br>Nembutal<br>Seconal<br>sedative-hypnotics:<br>Ativan<br>benzodiazepine<br>chloral hydate<br>Clonazapam (and<br> any other "...pam")<br>Dalmane<br>Equinil<br>Halcion<br>Dlonopin<br>Librax<br>Librium<br>Miltown<br>Placydil<br>Rostoril<br>Valium<br>Xanax | opiods:<br>codeine<br>Darvocet<br>Darvon<br>Demerol<br>Dilaudid<br>hydromorphone<br>hydrocodone<br>Lorcet<br>Lortab<br>methadone<br>Oxycontin<br>Tylenol with<br> codeine<br>Vicodin<br>Vicodin ES |
| Illegal | methamphetamine<br>cocaine | Mathaqualone<br>(quaaludes) | Opiates:<br>Opium<br>Heroin |

*With the exception of caffeine, all drugs listed can result in distortions and consequential destructive behaviors in susceptible individuals.

** Alcohol has attributes of all three of these classes of drugs, although it is considered by most to be a CNS (Central Nervous System) depressant.

# Myth #13
## "I don't use drugs. I only drink."

Alcohol is not only a drug capable of causing distortions of perception and memory, but it's also the first drug of choice for most addicted persons. If not, it's almost always one on which an addict will fall back if nothing else is readily available. And, it does more damage than all the other drugs combined.

The reason for the long-term harm is a result of the effect it has on neurotransmitter activity. Like similar drugs, it either directly revs up or disables the brakes on the "feel-good" neurotransmitters, those in the brain that contribute to general sedation, relaxation, calm feelings, stimulation, alleviation of depression and increasing self-confidence. However, while other drugs are laser-like in their affect on the neurotransmitters, alcohol takes a shotgun approach, affecting them all but not as powerfully. This allows the addict to continue using for decades even while appearing to be "functional," long after the life of the heroin addict has fallen apart.

## The Shotgun Approach is Longer Lasting

|          | Disables glutamate | Increases GABA | Boosts Dopamine | Releases Endorphins | Boosts Seratonin |
|----------|:---:|:---:|:---:|:---:|:---:|
| Alcohol  | X | X | X | X | X |
| Sedatives | X |   |   |   |   |
| Valium   |   | X |   |   |   |
| Cocaine  |   |   | X |   |   |
| Heroin   |   |   |   | X |   |
| Prozac   |   |   |   |   | X |

The disabling of glutamate by as much as 80% after as few as two drinks in the space of an hour leads to relaxation and general sedation, contributing to dis-coordination. The increase in GABA (gamma-aminobutyric acid) results in a pleasurable feeling of calm similar to Valium. The boost in dopamine provides enough stimulation to initially offset the depressant effects caused by the disabling of glutamate and increase in

GABA. The release of endorphins increases the body's painkillers and the boosting of serotonin alleviates depression while increasing self-confidence. Not only is alcohol a drug, but also an extraordinarily complex one.

In her autobiography, actress Patty Duke publicly aired this myth and took it even further. Her obviously alcoholic business managers gave her Bloody Marys at the age of 13 or 14. She later took Phenobarbital, Percodan, Thorazine, Stelazine, Valium, Seconal and other tranquilizers and in her twenties repeatedly got drunk, to the point of being "hung over most of the day because I drank most of the night."[16] Yet, she denied ever taking "drugs."

## Myth #14
## "Use of so-called 'hard' drugs causes far more destructive behaviors than does alcohol."

While researchers may disagree among themselves, every study has shown a greater level of violence among those using alcohol than other drug users. One concluded there was no significant evidence linking any drug except alcohol to violence.[17] Other studies have found that sedatives rank after alcohol as the drug most used prior to committing violence, followed by stimulants. Heroin addicts with ample supplies of their drug have been found unlikely to engage in physical abuse. Those using hallucinogens almost never do so. Marijuana users have been found underrepresented in the unlawful exercise of physical force, especially when compared to those under the influence of alcohol, barbiturates or amphetamines.[18] Furthermore, legal drugs were more likely to be associated with violence than were illegal ones.

On the other hand, the fact that cocaine is shorter acting than amphetamines results in greater levels of violence among amphetamine addicts than cocaine addicts.[19] The war on drugs, initially making it more difficult to obtain cocaine from overseas producers, resulted in a huge increase in the manufacture of locally produced amphetamines. The same is true for crack cocaine, which may exist only because of drug laws. As journalist Richard Cowan points out, "the more intense the law enforcement, the more potent the drugs will become."[20] In a classic twist in the law of unintended consequences, far less violence would be attributable to the other drugs were it not for prohibition creating this distortion in demand.

More important, 80 to 90% of mortality and crime resulting from illegal drugs is caused by other unintended consequences of prohibition, including turf battles and a need to steal to fund the addiction, while no more than 20% results from the biochemistry itself. Obviously, since alcohol is legal, virtually 100% of crime resulting from alcoholism is a result of its biochemistry. It would seem likely, then, that crime and mortality attributed to the intrinsic effects of illegal drugs are vastly overstated compared to the results of legal ones, including alcohol. This is supported in mortality studies, which show that for every death caused by the inherent effects of cocaine, heroin kills 20 and alcohol 37.[21] With few exceptions, only addicts regularly use drugs for which society imposes severe penalties for mere possession. Almost all who die from the intrinsic effects of alcohol are alcoholics. It is not a stretch to conclude, then, that the death rate from alcohol *addiction* is 37 times greater than the death rate from heroin addiction and nearly twice as great as deaths caused by the inherent effects of cocaine.

## Myth #15
## "Drugs create addicts by transforming their brains."

As previously described, the brain chemistry of addicts is different from that of non-addicts. This not only allows alcoholics to drink copiously without pain, but also motivates them to do so from the first time they put a drink to their lips.

The brain slowly undergoes further changes during active addiction. Neurotransmitter activity eventually begins to decline. This occurs relatively quickly when using drugs that target specific neurotransmitters in laser-like fashion, including heroin, Vicodin, Valium and cocaine. It can take decades when only alcohol is used because, while taking a shotgun approach and affecting all the neurotransmitters, its action on each is far weaker.

In isolated cases, non-addicts are given tranquilizers or other drugs on which they become physically dependent. Not predisposed to addiction, such patients are able to more quickly and easily stop using than are the biologically prone. Nor are they likely to relapse. Typically, they don't use their drugs in amounts significantly greater than that prescribed. If we were to identify these people as addicts, we would be stretching the meaning of the word. To increase the efficiency of language, the term "addict" should be employed only to describe those who engage in destructive behaviors as a result of use. Using this definition, drugs cannot create addicts but instead trigger addiction in those susceptible.

# Myth #16
## "Every drinker is a potential drunkard."

Recall the simple feedback mechanism in the brain of the non-alcoholic. At relatively benign BALs his body tells him, "slow it down, bud. You're drinking too much." This protects him from greatly diminishing his brain's ability to produce neurotransmitters.

To become a street drunk, the person with alcoholism needs to be able to drink enough of the drug to eventually impair the brain's capacity to produce its own neurotransmitters. This usually takes decades and cannot occur without heavy drinking for extended periods. (This may account for the fact that the "binge" drinker rarely if ever develops latter-stage alcoholism—he doesn't drink often enough to seriously impair neurotransmitter activity. Soviet tyrant Joseph Stalin, who lived to age 73, was such a drinker.) Heavy drinking cannot take place without the body being able to handle it, which occurs during early- to middle-stage alcoholism when the liver converts alcohol quickly into acetaldehyde and slowly into acetate. This is the biochemistry that makes a progression into latter-stage alcoholism possible. Only then does the brain crave a continuous flow of the drug, turning the hidden alcoholic into an obvious drunk.

Some suggest that the biochemistry doesn't explain the occasional older person who, after taking his first drink, quickly develops late-stage alcoholism. We don't yet fully understand all nuances of the biochemistry, with probably only 80 or 90% of it falling within our intellectual grasp. We'll leave science to discover the explanation for the few exceptions to the rule. In the meantime, the ability to explain and predict behaviors using the theories and research presented in this book is unparalleled and can be used to regain sanity as well as save millions of lives.

## Myth #17 (a "half-truth") "He drinks to escape."

This statement suggests that the need to escape causes alcoholism, which is another pernicious myth that even recovering alcoholics believe. Charlie Sheen is not the only one to have said, "I started using liquor and drugs as an escape."[22]

Recovering alcoholics often fail to understand the biological roots of their own alcoholism. Confusing correlation with causation should, then, not be surprising. Alcoholics *can* use alcohol and other drugs to numb their emotions. However, they *start* using addictively because their particular biochemistry allows it. They *continue* to do so because they can, which happens to allow them to engage in a form of "escape," probably caused by the distortions in memory symptomatic of alcoholism: euphoric recall, memory repression and blackouts.

## Myth #18 "She drinks because she's unhappy."

This is one of the most common and dangerous assumptions

made by many non-addicts.

If life's problems caused alcoholism, we'd all be alcoholics. When not viewed as challenges to overcome, problems and difficulties may trigger relapses into the disease, but they cannot cause it. Misery does not change the rate of conversion of alcohol into acetaldehyde and acetate.

Yet, our brains produce vast numbers and quantities of pharmaceutical-grade drugs. There is no doubt that we can change our biochemistry by smiling and frowning. While we can do so to a more significant degree via meditation, yoga and similar techniques, even these do not change the biochemistry of alcoholism. Many recovering alcoholics hope and try, but these attempts are based on rationalizations. Why do they even try at all? If alcohol were unimportant, they wouldn't bother. The problem is, alcoholics dream of drinking non-addictively while experiencing the unparalleled pleasure from use that only they can feel. However, while they can sometimes drink without observable adverse effects on their behaviors for a period of time, there are few if any reports of instances in which alcoholics have been able to continue to do so for more than a few years. Eventually, their innate biochemistry takes over. Sooner or later, the practicing alcoholic again becomes destructive, both of others and self.

Instead, the reverse of this statement is often true: she's unhappy because she drinks addictively. Alcoholism is often mistaken for Depressive Personality Disorder. According to studies, 50 to 80% of what appear to be Personality Disorders vanishes within three months of sobriety.[23] Therefore, such Disorders, including those manifesting as unhappiness, are more often than not symptoms of alcoholism.

## Myth #19
## "Some drink excessively to compensate for their shyness."

This doesn't account for the fact that many gregarious children later trigger alcoholism and most shy people are not alcoholics.

We *can* say that some shy people have a biological predisposition to alcoholism and use the excessive drinking to compensate for shyness, but only because they can. The reason is that the simple biochemistry, which allows them to drink addictively, makes them feel invincible, resulting in a sense that they can do no wrong. This feeling can take form in observably loquacious or boisterous behaviors, such as those often found in bars or at parties.

## Myth #20
## "Excessive drinking can make up for a lack of self-esteem."

Ask a recovering alcoholic if he drank because he was unhappy. With five or ten years of sobriety, he will admit that he drank because he's an alcoholic and the drinking created or contributed to his despair.

In the same way, while lacking self-esteem does not cause addictive drinking, alcoholism contributes to a decline in self-respect. With enough use and bad behaviors, such esteem is eventually zeroed out. This may be due to the fact that during periods of abstinence, when moments of clarity are occasionally experienced, alcoholics recollect some of their misbehaviors. In addition, negative outcomes of drinking episodes may be seen as irrefutable and inescapable proof of poor behaviors, even if the circumstances are not recalled. Such consequences could include harm to others resulting from accident or error.

If drinking compensated for a lack of self-esteem, continuous drinking would remedy the problem. The process of inflating the ego instead results in behaviors that contribute to its decline. Conversely, many non-alcoholics are unhappy and lack self-esteem. If such problems caused alcoholism, the disease would develop.

## Myth #21
## "I didn't experience any significant withdrawal symptoms when I quit drinking. Therefore, I can't possibly be an alcoholic."

Withdrawal symptoms generally occur only after decades of use. Using this as the criterion, no one could ever be identified as having early stage alcoholism.

This is the defense given by many alcoholics who stop drinking for periods of time. It doesn't preclude the possibility that the person is not an alcoholic; after all, if a person gave up drinking after having only a couple of drinks per night for a decade or longer, he's not going to experience withdrawal. On the other hand, why did he "give up" drinking? While he may in fact have been a light to moderate drinker, he may not have been. His "couple of drinks" might have been two 27-ounce Long Island iced teas.

Audrey Kishline, founder of "Moderation Management," a support group for problem drinkers attempting to moderate their drinking, emphasized this point in defending the idea that she couldn't possibly be an alcoholic. In a book in which she described the program, she recounted her experience when first admitted into an alcoholism treatment center: "It is important to note that *I did not experience any significant withdrawal symptoms when I quit drinking*," indicating that her physical dependence on alcohol was not "severe."[24] She was never told that decades of active alcoholism are usually required before physical dependence occurs and that such dependence is but one *symptom* of latter-stage alcoholism.

## Myth #22
## "Because the gene for alcoholism has never been located, there is no proof that alcoholism is a disease."

The fact that the gene has not yet been found is often used to support the idea that there is no disease of "excessive drinking." However, something, activated by drinking alcoholic beverages, causes brain damage, resulting in poor behaviors. The circumstantial evidence for the hypothesis that this is caused by a differential processing of the drug is overwhelming. Those waiting for absolute proof may wait decades, all the while suffering from active alcoholism in themselves or others and making the lives of close persons a living hell. In the meantime, billions of lies will be told, millions of relationships ruined and hundreds of thousands of lives destroyed every year.

The germs causing puerperal fever were not identified until thirty years after Dr. Ignas Semmelweis announced that millions of mothers and babies died because doctors didn't wash their hands before delivery. Few medical professionals listened to his plea to scrub after operations and visits to the morgue. He was ignored even as his clinic experienced death rates a fraction of others all over Europe during the mid-1800s. Only after Louis Pasteur convinced doctors that the late Semmelweis was right, did doctors begin washing up between operations and after handling corpses.

As wind whistles through pine trees even when no one hears it, germs exist though invisible. As the circumstantial evidence of trees blown over and illness and death from germs is observable, so are the effects of alcoholism in awful behaviors. This is true even though we have not yet found the gene.

## Myth #23 (a "half-truth")
## "Smoking is more dangerous than drinking alcohol."

Smoking is harmful to those who smoke. While more deadly to the non-alcoholic than drinking, using alcohol addictively is potentially lethal not only to the addict, but also to everyone around him.

Society attacks smoking, an addiction that aside from the smoke (from which we can easily escape) kills only the smoker. Alcoholism kills, mutilates and otherwise harms billions of others. Its biochemistry causes the afflicted to lie, betray, cheat and embezzle. It makes people act in ways that destroy countless family, personal, business and professional relationships. Yet, the war on tobacco gets the headlines.

Not that we need a war on alcohol, or any other drug. Nothing keeps an addict from his drug, if that's what he wants. We need instead to concentrate on behaviors associated with use. If a person's misbehaviors can be connected in this way, society, employers, insurers, creditors and/or family have a right to proscribe use by that person as a condition of freedom, employment, insurability, obtaining a loan or remaining in a relationship.

## Myth #24
## "He really knows better. He knows what he did and knows he is at fault."

Alcoholics experience three key distortions of perception. One is the aforementioned "euphoric recall." Among other impairments, this leads to rationalizations that allow justification for all misbehaviors, including gross dishonesty. However, since this distortion causes the afflicted to believe he is always right, he has no conscious knowledge of lying.

The second is "memory repression." While the alcoholic eventually recollects such memories, it may take years or decades. In the meantime, such memories are inaccessible to him.

The third is the aforementioned "blackout." Recall that blackouts are not simply conking out. They are instead chemically induced occasions during which events and actions do not enter the memory bank even though the person appears wide-awake. As far as the alcoholic is concerned, anything that occurs during a blackout never happened.

Recovering alcoholics claim to be the world's greatest liars when in their diseased state. A common refrain at Alcoholics Anonymous meetings is "when we were using, we could sell ice to Eskimos." And indeed, they could. There is no sneakier way for the non-violent alcoholic to wield power over others than by lying. However, ego inflation is not the only reason behind what appear to be lies. Alcoholics can experience black-outs for days at a time. In recovery, some tell us they remember little or nothing of events that occurred during most of their drinking career. In addition, they may distort the truth subconsciously. So, while there is an appearance of lying, it may be unintentional.

## Myth #25 (a "half-truth")
## "O.J. knows what he did."

O.J. Simpson has on numerous occasions publicly exhibited behavioral indications of alcoholism. In 1989 he even wrote a note to then wife Nicole Brown Simpson in which he apologized for committing an act of domestic violence, adding, "...I'm not going to blame being drunk...." He told her he would stop drinking and join AA.[25]

While O.J. and others like him may be aware of their heinous crimes and seemingly have no remorse due to rationalizations based on the subconscious belief that they are gods, they may simply not recollect the events. The result is the same: no remorse and what appears to be an extraordinary ability to convincingly lie. Oddly, it may not be lying: an alleged murderer may simply not remember that he did it.

"[The youths who, in the study,] grew up in intact families but with alcoholic biological parents were at four or five times greater risk of developing alcoholism than those who grew up in severely disrupted families but did not have an alcoholic biological parent. In other words, parental conflict is associated with greater risk of alcoholism only when that conflict is an indicator of parental alcoholism."

—George E. Vaillant[26]

# 2

# Environment, Circumstances, Personality & Gender

## Myth #26
## "Alcoholism is both genetic *and* environmental."

What role does the environment play in determining one's initial biochemistry? If none, the inception of alcoholism is not "genetic *and* environmental." Since the alcoholic's biochemistry is different, it must be in the genes.

Alcoholism tends to run in some families far more than in others. It seems that the longer one's ancestors have had access to fermented grains and fruit in large quantities, the lower the likelihood of inheriting alcoholism. With exposure, comes resistance. Mediterranean populations, which may have had access to fermented substances for over 10,000 years, have a relatively low rate of alcoholism, estimated at 5 to 10%. Northern Europeans, by contrast, with access for no more than 1,500 years, have a rate estimated at 20 to 30%. North American Native Americans, with almost no access to fermented grains and fruits in large quantities until the last 400 years, have virtually no resistance to alcoholism and, as a result, suffer from rates as high as 75%.

"Environmental" gives rise to the possibility that alcoholics can "unlearn" their alcoholism. There are no recorded long-term instances of this occurring. It also suggests that morality may have something to do with its inception, since one's moral beliefs are largely a product of one's environment. There is, then, an implication that those with alcoholism — including as many as three-quarters of Native Americans — are "bad" people. This creates a stigma so great that many prefer the assumption that a person exhibiting rotten behaviors is simply "bad" rather than the assertion that, God forbid, alcoholism might explain the conduct. The idea that the predisposition to alcoholism is 100% genetically determined goes far in removing this stigma.

Donald Goodwin, M.D., conducted a study of alcoholism in brothers who were sons of alcoholics. One son in each set was raised in the alcoholic family while the other was adopted out within weeks of birth and brought up by unrelated parents. If environmental factors such as alcoholism in the custodial parent were controlling, we would find a far higher rate of alcoholism among the sons raised in the alcoholic home than in the non-alcoholic one. Instead, *there was no difference in the incidence of alcoholism between the two groups of brothers*, which was four times the rate found in the overall population.[27] This shatters the idea that the genesis of alcoholism is in any way related to environmental influences.

This should not be confused with the *form* that alcoholism takes, which is a function of environment and other factors. Some alcoholics are far more destructive than others. The style of destruction varies tremendously based on circumstances, environment and underlying Psychological Type and Temperament. However, these are not the triggers for alcoholic biochemistry.

# Myth #27
# "Proper parenting and involvement will prevent alcoholism."

Good parenting seems to be correlated with the prevention of not only alcohol and other drug addiction, but also even use. However, studies fail to point to the more likely underlying connection: good parents are not practicing alcoholics.

Parents who are practicing alcoholics have a love affair with a drug. This precludes appropriate and healthy love for another human being. Recovering alcoholics with long-term sobriety admit to psychological abandonment and abuse of children, spouse and significant others, all of whom agree with this assessment. The drug, if not the addict himself, is the center of the addict's life, around which everything else revolves. Practicing alcoholics, therefore, are far less likely to involve themselves with family concerns than are non-alcoholics or recovering ones. Proper parenting and involvement are, then, indicative of non-alcoholic parents passing non-alcoholic genes to their children.

Since the likelihood of a child inheriting alcoholism is far lower when parents are not addicts, these children are more likely to become healthy non-addict adults. The surprise occurs when a child with a good upbringing develops alcoholism. The explanation lies in the inherited biochemistry of processing the drug and in the fact that it may not act upon that generation, just as hair color, eye color and dimples may "skip" generations. Once a child with alcoholic biochemistry begins drinking, alcoholism will be triggered regardless of the number of baseball games or school events that parents and children attend together.

Good parenting may delay the onset of alcoholism in the predisposed, since there are fewer chances to experiment and addict friends with whom to associate. This in itself can be helpful, but not preventive. Stories abound of alcoholics triggering their disease in their 20s and 30s, long out of school, running successful businesses and already devoted spouses and parents themselves. Innate biochemistry explains this; upbringing does not.

# Myth #28
## "If he'd had a better upbringing, he wouldn't be an alcoholic."

Since the overall odds of alcoholism in the United States are about 10%, we can extrapolate from Dr. Goodwin's studies that the likelihood of a child of an alcoholic inheriting the disease is about 40%. It's also reasonable to reverse the idea: a child who is an alcoholic is more likely to have an alcoholic parent. Two studies of female alcoholics, in which 41% and 49% had at least one alcoholic parent supports this idea.[28]

Since alcoholism in a parent *always* leads to some form of abuse (even if only verbal disparaging or psychological abandonment) and instability, a psychologically healthy, stable upbringing is rare for the alcoholic with or without celebrity status. Since non-alcoholic children often adopt some of their alcoholic parents' inappropriate behaviors, a truly healthy upbringing even for grandchildren of alcoholics could be rare. Hence, the difficulty in finding public examples of alcoholics who grew up in good families. In addition, since most biographers haven't a clue as to the importance of alcoholism in explaining the behaviors of their subjects, little or nothing may be offered about the possibility of its existence in the person under scrutiny, much less the parents or grandparents. Further, the stigma of alcoholism and enabling by close persons, especially of the wealthy and powerful (the usual subject of biographies), makes it difficult to obtain such information. This can be true even for the knowledgeable biographer.

On the other hand, although scarce, there are a few public reports of children walking out of the best of homes and schools with addiction. One well-known example is President George W. Bush. No one would deny the excellence of his upbringing and yet he told Barbara Walters that his wife Laura gave him a choice at age 40 between Jack Daniels and her. He made the right decision.

Unfortunately, the Bush daughters exhibit behavioral indications of alcoholism and again, evidence suggests they have had an excellent upbringing and attended good schools. Public information on his brother, Governor Jeb Bush of Florida, suggests that he does not have alcoholism. However, his daughter Noelle, arrested for prescription fraud on January 29, 2002, is clearly afflicted with this disease. Hers is not likely a case of parental ineptitude.

Retrospective behavioral studies query people about their past. Prospective ones, which ignore everything prior to the beginning of the study, follow subjects, interviewing them numerous times, often over decades. Because the alcoholic's memory cannot be relied on due to the distortions caused by euphoric recall, memory repression and blackouts, retrospective studies of alcoholics are useless. Long-term prospective studies are, therefore, essential to studying alcoholism, gaining an understanding of the disease, its progression and the truth about events that occur in the lives of alcoholics.[29]

In one such study involving several hundred men, a psychologist interviewed a subject, James, at age 18. The psychologist reported that the young man had a warm home with good peer relations and little conflict with his parents, who were deemed reliable, consistent and devoted. The childhood environment was rated in the top third of the group studied. He predicted that James would develop into a hard working, non-alcoholic citizen. However, by his late 20s while writing his Ph.D. thesis, James was drinking constantly. He became a member of AA at age 52.

Martha Morrison, an active addict by age 12, reports in her autobiography *White Rabbit* that her family was basically stable, happy and free of conflict. She suffered no emotional problems prior to triggering her addiction. As a child, she never lacked material comforts and "was probably fairly spoiled..."[30] By age 17, she was consuming 20 different drugs a day, continuing at roughly that pace until two years into her residency as a psychiatrist.

Few would suggest that members of the Kennedy clan have had poor upbringings, yet alcoholism is epidemic in their family. One tragic example was that of Michael Kennedy, son of the late Senator Robert F. Kennedy. After admitting to an affair with a 14-year old teenage girl who babysat his children, he explained that the "incident was caused by a drinking problem," and enrolled in an alcohol rehabilitation program.[31] He died soon after in a skiing accident in Aspen, Colorado, which may also have been alcohol-related. Another is that of Michael Skakel, a nephew of Robert F. Kennedy's widow, convicted of slaying Martha Moxley in 1975 when he was only 15 years old. Since he was enrolled in a substance abuse treatment center during the 1970s, active addiction could account for the backdrop behind the professed motive reported by a classmate during the trial: that Skakel's brother "stole his girlfriend.[32]" Violence is a common response by alcoholics whose egos are under attack.

William C. Moyers, son of television journalist Bill Moyers, was raised comfortably in good surroundings in the Long Island suburb of Garden City. He went to decent public schools, regularly attended church and had to earn his spending money. He admits this his parents raised him "to become the best child I could." The young Moyers ran marathons as captain of the high school track team and played trombone in the school band. Yet, by his early 20s, William Moyers was "addicted to pretty much everything and anything."[33] It took several long stays in rehab to get clean and sober.

On the other hand, we often don't know that the truth of the matter is opposite to the reports of an alcoholic. At age 36 James, the young man in the long-term study, told researchers that his parents had been cold. The late alcohol-addict producer Don Simpson told *Smart* magazine in 1990 that his father "used to pick me up and throw me against the wall, and as I hit the ground, he'd kick me." His mother, he said, was "very manipulative and very narrow-minded." Friends who met his parents at Simpson's memorial were reported as "pleasantly surprised when they seemed to be perfectly nice people who were proud of their son." One woman said, "She was a darling woman." As another friend put it, "There was always the Don Simpson discount factor," never knowing if he was telling the truth about his parents "or, for that matter, anything else."[34]

## Myth #29
## "Since 60% of children of alcoholics do *not* develop alcoholism, we can conclude that the disease is not genetically-determined."

If true, there would be few, if any, genetically determined diseases. We would, under this standard, need a higher level of inheritance to qualify a disease as genetic. According to some, it seems that nothing less than a 100% incidence of inheritance entitles us to conclude that a disease is genetically based.[35]

Yet, many diseases and disorders that pass through to a small number of one's progeny have genetic origins, including diabetes, sickle-cell anemia, Tay-Sachs and hemophilia. The fact that few inherit these diseases does not mean they are not genetic.

The fact that we have not yet found the gene responsible for alcoholism may seem baffling, until we understand that few with early-stage alcoholism are identified as such. Further, none are "alcoholics" until in recovery. It's difficult to study those in whom a disease is not diagnosed and who are incapable of self-identification.

## Myth #30
## "Poor upbringing, environment, circumstances or a combination of these cause alcoholism."

We often hear, "Oh that Johnny! How could he use drugs? He's from such a fine family!" Johnny uses because peer pressure, curiosity and ready availability combine to up the odds of experimentation. The first drug is often alcohol, because it is so often found in the parents' (or a friend's parents') liquor cabinet. If a predisposition is inherited and even moderate use occurs, alcoholism will be triggered.

If poor upbringing caused the disease, adolescents wouldn't walk out of Beverly Hills High School as full-blown addicts. We wouldn't find families in which only one of six siblings has alcoholism, or five of six. After all, children in the same family have essentially the same environment, whether or not a healthy one, while living at home. Many raised in terrible conditions do not develop alcoholism while some with excellent upbringings do. Further, there are no studies showing a correlation between birth order and incidence of alcoholism.

While environment can alter biochemistry, it usually does so only after decades, as in the case of carcinogenic substances eventually causing cancer. Alcoholism, on the other hand, is generally triggered during the first drinking episode. It is unlikely that environment can alter a biochemistry this deep-rooted.

Furthermore, many alcoholics remember their first drinking occasion, while non-alcoholics rarely do. What could be so important to the incipient addict that would cause him to recall such a seemingly unimportant event? The extraordinary experience at the get-go seems to implant the incident permanently in the memory. At the other end of the spectrum, as author James Graham points out, the fact that alcoholism in some isn't triggered until taking a first drink at an advanced age is "incompatible with any notion that addiction is caused by environmental factors."[36]

If environment and other circumstances caused alcoholism, alcoholics could learn to drink non-addictively by changing their surroundings. With so many attempting this, those in recovery long ago coined a phrase, "pulling a geographic," to describe a change of residence in the hope of effecting a cure. However, there are no reported instances in which alcoholics have learned to drink without eventually acting destructively. This includes even those retiring to relatively stress-free locales such as tropical islands.

## Myth #31
### "She was a victim of incest, beatings, or other child-abuse; no wonder she's an alcoholic."

Being such a victim is compelling evidence that the person committing the crime has alcoholism. One expert on incest, Wendy Maltz, explains that "*Sexual abuse occurs whenever one person dominates and exploits another by means of sexual activity or suggestion.* Sexual feelings and behavior are used to degrade, humiliate, control, hurt, or otherwise misuse another person. Coercion or betrayal often play into sexual abuse."[37] Many recovering alcoholics include such misbehaviors when "taking inventory," a necessary pre-condition for making amends to the victims of such conduct.

42

While difficult to obtain statistics on the percentage of such crimes committed by alcoholics, anecdotal evidence suggests that 80 to 90% of those inflicting such abuse have alcoholism. Most of the rest, as is the case for the sexually compulsive, may be children of alcoholics who have learned particularly heinous behaviors.

Why do so many victims develop the disease? Consider Goodwin's studies, which found that the odds of a child of an alcoholic inheriting alcoholism are four times that of the overall population. They develop it because they were genetically predisposed. On the other hand, many victims never become alcoholics. Alcoholism fails to pass through to about 60% of children of alcoholics, regardless of the degree of parental abuse.

## Myth #32
## "The stresses of the job and other life problems made her turn to the bottle."

When six-time Grammy winner Whitney Houston entered rehab in March 2004 her spiritual adviser, Prince Asiel Ben Israel, explained to the audience on CBS' "The Early Show" that her "drug problem is the result of living a high-pressure celebrity life."[38] However, if life's problems caused alcoholism, we'd all be alcoholics. Many entertainers are addicts; *most* are not. Those who can use to relieve perceived stress, do so. Those for whom such use cannot relieve stress may try to use addictively, but no matter how hard they try, they will fail.

Ironically, alcoholics only *think* they can relieve stress by using alcohol. This belief results from distortions in perceptions, which lead to impaired thinking. As suggested by the "Survival Games" (ways of coping in social environments perceived to be threatening) in which alcoholics engage, having an appearance of Personality Disorders, alcoholism *causes* enormous stress.

The late alcoholism authority Vernon E. Johnson found

after decades of working with alcoholics that "alcoholism cannot exist unless there is a conflict between the values and behavior of the drinker."[39] This suggests that alcoholics *always* violate their underlying core (non-alcoholic) values when active in their disease. Violation of core values *always* puts the person under intense stress. This, in turn, *always* causes him to play Survival Games. *Therefore, playing Survival Games is not only an excellent clue to alcoholism, but also suggests that there is intense stress.* It appears to feed on itself, so that alcoholism causes stress and stress aggravates (but does not initiate) alcoholism.

## Myth #33 (a "half-truth")
## "The younger a person begins drinking, the more likely alcoholism is to develop."

Technically, this is correct. Forty percent of children who start drinking by age 14 will trigger alcoholism, compared with 25% of adolescents who begin at age 17 and 10% of young adults whose first drink is taken at ages 21 and 22.[40] However, correlation is not causation. Easy access by young children of alcoholics in which the disease runs in the family likely allows these children to trigger an incipient alcoholism at younger ages.

This is not to suggest that we shouldn't try to delay onset. It's possible that a few budding alcoholics, knowing the history of alcoholism in their family, take a drink and, instantly sensing how it makes them feel or seeing the results of how it made them act, stop right then and there. Consciously making a decision to not drink for this reason is more likely to occur at an older age than in adolescence, if it happens at all. On the other hand, those triggering alcoholism post-adolescence may be less likely to exhibit obvious signs of alcoholism and, therefore, may be less likely identified as such. Despite this possibility, longitudinal studies showing that Drug Abuse Resistance Education (D.A.R.E.) doesn't decrease drug use over the long-term suggest that the incidence of alcohol and other drug addiction has nothing to do with the age at which one takes his first drink, hit, snort or line.

# Myth #34
## "We can teach kids not to use drugs."

Were it only that easy. The ready availability, particularly of alcohol, almost precludes the possibility of the predisposed person never triggering a drug addiction, especially to alcohol. While we can teach safe use of firearms, we cannot teach the person biologically predisposed to addiction how to safely use drugs or to say "no" once the use begins. Therefore, we might instead teach kids that if they use, some will trigger alcoholism, many of whom will be "functioning" for decades, while others will quickly graduate to other drugs, *usually* becoming less functional early on. In either case, they will eventually ruin relationships, betray friends or destroy lives. The afflicted person will, over the long run, be the last to grasp the idea that his own addiction wreaks havoc on many with whom he comes into contact, even those he may love, when sober.

We can also teach children to identify clues to addiction in friends. After all, these are "friends" only as long as the codependent, or close person, does the addict's bidding. We might teach parents that their child would indeed engage in vile or bizarre behaviors if alcoholism has been triggered. We could instruct educators that repeated adolescent misbehaviors are often symptoms of a deeper underlying problem having *nothing* to do with environment.

We can then give young people the support needed to inflict consequences on friends in whom addiction has been tentatively identified. This requires a new educational paradigm in which everyone is taught to say "no" to the addicts in their lives and the idea that "friends don't tell on friends" is reversed, bringing an end to the "code of silence" prevalent among both children and adults. While we will rarely prevent use, we can proactively intervene at or near the inception by imposing responsibility for misbehaviors and coercing the addict into abstinence, hopefully *before* tragedy happens.

## Myth #35
## "We can prevent use through education, thereby decreasing the number of addicts."

Almost all attempts at this have failed. As mentioned, long-term studies of D.A.R.E. have shown that its approach doesn't work.[41] Much of the reason for failure may have to do with its focus on the drug, rather than the person on the drug. In addition, failure is inevitable in a society in which sooner or later almost every adolescent experiments, thereby triggering addiction in the predisposed. If we show children that alcoholism runs in families, we *may* be able to prevent use by those having a higher probability of inheriting a predisposition to alcoholism.

Studies reporting positive results for D.A.R.E. have measured only the program's short-term success rate. Many Drug Recognition Experts, the law enforcement drug specialists, agree that such programs have had no significant long-term affect on use. If we stop preaching that drugs are evil and get honest by teaching that most can use alcohol safely and only a few cannot, we might have greater success. Most non-alcoholics can use other drugs, especially the heavily advertised pharmaceuticals, without acting destructively. In addition, we misleadingly recommend that drinkers "use alcohol in moderation." There is no such thing as long-term moderation for an addict. The non-addict exercises restraint in the long run, because his body's feedback requires him to do so. Therefore, we preach to the choir.

Further, anti-drug advertising has been reported a failure by no less than U.S. drug czar, John P. Walters.[42] A five-year-old anti-drug campaign, developed by top Madison Avenue ad agencies, was considered a novel and revolutionary step. An evaluation of the campaign showed that it not only failed in decreasing drug use, but also may have even increased use among adolescents. The ads attempted both soft and harsh approaches ranging from visuals showing that hobbies such as art can be a natural high, to showing a doped-up addict wasting away. Sober people would think that such an approach would have positive outcomes, but their perceptions are not distorted.

Another method of advertising, directed at college students, also flopped. The "social norms marketing" technique tried to reduce drinking by showing students how little their peers drink. It, too, failed and may have even contributed to an increase in drinking by informing students who don't drink at all that they are abnormal. While one college reported some success with the method, the study reporting it a failure included 35,000 students on more than 100 campuses. Perhaps the one school where it seems to have helped combined this method with other unreported techniques.[43]

This doesn't mean an ad campaign that accomplishes its goal of reducing drug use and, therefore, the triggering of incipient addiction cannot be created. However, the efforts so far suggest that we should concentrate on early intervention rather than prevention, with promises of consequences for misbehaviors rather than use. One such program didn't say a word about safety or death tolls on the road. It didn't show an ambulance or repeat the "Friends Don't Let Friends Drive Drunk" slogan. Instead, it showed cops arresting drivers. The ad campaign was run nationwide because a program on which it was based in Tennessee is believed to have reduced alcohol-related incidents by 20%. This approach demonstrated that increasing the likelihood of legal consequences, including loss of license and jail-time, could be effective.[44] Its relative success may be due to appealing to the survival instinct of the lower brain centers, as opposed to a futile attempt at reason.

We can't teach those with a damaged neo-cortex that a drug which makes the user feel like he is God is somehow bad for him. On the other hand, an ad campaign that focuses on educating non-addicts about the disease has never been tried. Ads could show recovering alcoholics thanking those who helped them experience an arrest for DUI or temporary loss of family, while describing why pain from appropriate and logical consequences got them sober before they killed someone or ruined yet another relationship. A public service announcement might portray recovering alcoholics refusing liquor, explaining that their particular biochemistry causes misbehaviors when they drink. Still another might depict recovering addicts telling the audience that if they had been in a position of power while using, they would have been capable of *any* behavior. A video might include images of tyrants, mass murderers or less destructive well-known alcoholics who married and divorced several times: just imagine what must have been happening behind closed doors.

## Myth #36
## "Since advertising alcohol increases use, it should be banned!"

The former Soviet Union allowed no advertising of alcoholic beverages (or anything else) for 70 years. Various degrees of prohibition, generally focusing on restricting supplies, were attempted several times, with all efforts failing. The area has suffered and still endures disastrously high rates of alcoholism.

When the United States attempted Prohibition, advertising was banned. While overall use declined, consumption is believed to have remained stable among those who needed to stop using. The results of this failed experiment are well known.

While advertising may increase use by non-alcoholics and cause buyers of all stripes to switch brands, it has not been shown to do more than this. If directed at children it *could* trigger drinking and, therefore, alcoholism at a younger age, but even this has never been proven. The more likely initiation to drinking is a child's own drinking parents, alcoholic or not.

Prohibition is far more extreme than a mere ban on advertising. If such bans worked, prohibition should do a far better job. Not only did Prohibition fail in the United States, but also in every country in which it has been tried. China is said to have attempted it seventeen times and England six. Finland and Iceland have each initiated and repealed prohibition at least once.[45] If general prohibition reduced use by addicts, a result that could eliminate 80% of mankind's troubles in one fell-swoop, it wouldn't be repealed. However, such bans fall short because they spread enforcement too thin, open the floodgates to corruption and lack the moral strength provided by connecting use to poor behaviors. If, instead, we target the relatively few who create problems for others — the person, not the drug — there is a far greater chance of stopping the use where it matters.

## Myth #37
## "Some Personality Types are more likely to be alcoholics."

Personality Type, along with virulence, circumstances and environment, determine the form that addiction takes. However, the roots of alcoholism are in the biochemistry. It seems unlikely that the gene causing alcoholism is somehow related to the gene determining core personality.

The personality classification that many believe is the most useful in terms of predicting and explaining healthy human behavior is the Myers-Briggs Personality Type Indicator in conjunction with Keirseyan Temperament Theory. Psychologist David Keirsey integrated Myers-Briggs with the four basic human Temperaments, as depicted in various forms for thousands of years.[46] These describe one's source of self-esteem, values and underlying core needs. Since Temperament is correlated with Survival Games, which are, in turn, similar in appearance to Personality Disorders, these can be useful in predicting and understanding unhealthy behaviors.

The difficulty in identifying certain people as alcoholics is that there are as many manifestations of alcoholism as there are addicts. Some are far less destructive than are others. This can be explained at least in part by comparing predicted Personality Disorders with Temperaments. For example, those of one particular Temperament have an underlying need to be free to act, often on impulse. When addicted, these types often look like Sociopaths. Those of a different Temperament, whose core needs include the acquisition of knowledge, wisdom and competencies, are often misdiagnosed while practicing alcoholics as having the (usually) relatively benign Obsessive-Compulsive Personality Disorder. Since the Sociopath is potentially far more dangerous to others than is the Obsessive, the former may be more easily diagnosed as alcoholic. Therefore, some personality types may only *appear* to have a higher predisposition to alcoholism than do others. Biochemistry is not likely to favor one Temperament over another. If true, addiction, like most every other disease, is an equal opportunity one in regards to underlying personality.

## Myth #38
## "A larger percentage of men are alcoholics."

This myth probably results in part from the fact that women, overall, drink smaller quantities of alcohol than do men. In addition, they are less likely to drink in public for fear of not appearing ladylike. This does not mean they have a lower incidence of alcoholism.

Recall that the amount of liquor needed to increase the BAL to a given point is a function mostly of the weight of the drinker. A 120-pound person needs one-third less alcohol than a 200-pounder to keep up. While the latter requires 12 drinks over four hours to reach a BAL of .18 per cent, the former needs only eight.

In addition, doctors often prescribe Xanax, Valium, tranquilizers, or barbiturates for women suffering from apparent emotional, mood or sleep disorders who should instead be treated for alcoholism. As a result, the Betty Ford Center estimates that up to 80% of female alcoholics are cross-addicted to pharmaceutical drugs. Because pills and alcohol "potentiate" each other, far less of each is needed to become intoxicated. For example, one-fifth of a potent dose of alcohol combined with a small amount of Valium is four to eight times stronger than the same amount of either drug by itself. Many alcoholics are thereby able to reach an alcoholic high with only a few drinks, which does not look like alcoholism. Even the close observer may not see the pills slipped in alongside the booze.

Furthermore, non-alcoholics commit very little violence post-adolescence. Over 85% of domestic abuse is committed by alcoholics.[47] What appears to be a preponderance of men perpetrating such violence seems to support the idea that the number of alcoholic men exceeds that of women. However, studies indicate that women initiate as much abuse as do men; it's just not as obvious because women are generally not as strong and most men are more able to protect themselves, resulting in a lower rate of injury. This, along with embarrassment and fear of ridicule over being beaten up by a woman, could account for the fact that men have been found to be nine times less likely to report abuse. Yet, wives commit half of spousal murders and weapons are more often used to make up for physical disadvantages in the initiation of violence. Further, mothers have been found to abuse their children at almost twice the rate of fathers.[48]

Other circumstantial evidence suggesting gross underestimates of the level of female abusers and, hence, lower addiction among women, is that, according to the U.S. Department of Justice, every year there are roughly 7,800 unsolved murders of men yet only 1,500 unsolved murders of women.[49] "Unsolved" includes acquittals. The same study reports that a woman is nine times more likely to be acquitted for the murder of a spouse than is a man. Therefore, there may be more female murderers than is accounted for in the statistics. One reason for failing to prove a greater number of murders of men when a woman could be culpable is what men's issues author Warren Farrell calls "blinders" to female murder of men. Commentator Glenn Sacks, explains that one of these blinders is the fact that women are sneakier than men. They more often poison the victim, death from which is often recorded as "heart attack" or "accident," and are more likely to use contract killers, who often disguise murders as accidents or suicides.[50]

Moreover, a man's lifetime risk of being struck by a partner is the same as a woman's, 28%. Domestic violence is roughly the same among lesbian, gay and heterosexual couples. As columnist Norah Vincent puts it, "women hit women too."[51]

Perhaps most damning, alcoholics who do not commit violence make up for it in other ways. Verbal abuse is very common, as are accusations that are later proved false. While alcoholic men commit most acts of rape, alcoholic women likely make a large preponderance of false accusations of rape. The challenge in determining the truth in these cases as in others brought before the criminal justice system is often in uncovering who is the alcohol or other drug addict. The evidence strongly suggests that the overall incidence of alcoholism between men and women is roughly equal in societies in which alcohol use by women is not strictly proscribed by male enforcers.

# 3

# Control over Use

**Myth #39 (a "half-truth")**
**"Alcoholics can learn to control their drinking."**

Alcoholics can control drinking in early-stage alcoholism for extended periods. However, such self-restraint is never permanent.

There have been many studies purporting to show that alcoholics can exercise such control. Perhaps the most famous of these is the study conducted by Mark and Linda Sobell from 1969 to 1971 at Patton State Hospital in California, in which an attempt was made to teach chronic alcoholics moderate drinking habits. After two years, they succeeded, or so it seemed. Thirty-five percent of their sample achieved "good" days, which were defined as less than seven ounces of 80-proof liquor a day, or about five standard drinks, for 98% of the year or better. A seemingly large 85% of the subjects had at least 85% "good" days.[52] However, no mention was made of the damage caused to relationships the other 15% of the time. Interestingly, most of the time they didn't drink at all, remaining abstinent more days than another group studied in which abstinence was the goal.[53] The Sobells didn't say whether temporary periods of abstinence might be due to the problems caused by poor behaviors on the 55 days of each year on which they drank the equivalent of five drinks or more. Quite simply, the study failed to measure behaviors, an improvement in which should be considered the litmus test for recovery. Nor did the study take into account the fact that alcoholism is a disease in which misbehaviors occur only *some* of the time.

Worse, the attempts at control were shown to have failed in a follow-up of the Sobells' subjects.[54] At the ten-year mark, nine of the 20 subjects had experienced at least intermittent damage from alcohol "abuse," four had died from alcohol-related causes and six had been abstinent for several years. Only one subject had continued drinking in a seemingly controlled manner for the entire 10-year period, and there was some question about whether this individual was actually alcoholic. As alcoholism authority George E. Vaillant points out, "it is not surprising that the lives of experimentally treated alcoholics would look very different in a 10-year study by critical outsiders than they did over two years to investigators intimately involved in the alcoholics' treatment." These results provide additional support for the idea that long-term prospective studies are crucial since alcoholics can control their drinking for extended periods, including many years.[55]

It is interesting that the Sobells never tried to replicate their own findings. Other long-term studies have had similar results to the follow-up of the Sobell research. In one,[56] researchers attempted to prove that alcoholics could control their drinking by using, according to Vaillant, "every technique known to behavior modification." At the end of nearly four years, every subject in the study had gotten drunk. The behaviors resulting from such drinking were apparently so bad that the researchers called off the experiment, announcing it would be unethical to continue. Another researcher found that after seven years only 1.6% of 1,289 diagnosed and treated alcoholics had become successful moderate drinkers. Of these, most showed few obvious symptoms of true alcoholism.[57]

Perhaps the most publicly tragic example of a person who successfully moderated her drinking for a number of years and then lost control is Audrey Kishline, founder of Moderation Management. She argued that "problem drinkers" could exercise self-restraint by taking responsibility for their behaviors.[58] After six years of apparent success, she experienced a loss of control and rejoined AA. After the incident in which she killed two others while driving under the influence, she was contrite and announced that Moderation Management "is nothing but alcoholics covering up their problem."[59]

Does this mean that those who could be identified as having alcoholism can never moderate their drinking? Not necessarily. A number of studies have shown that anywhere from barely over one percent to a bit over five per cent of "alcoholics" can learn to control use for extended periods. It may be that once someone has done this for ten years, then the drinking can be considered "safe." However, it is possible that some are misdiagnosed "alcoholic" from the start and that others, who engage in sporadically poor behaviors, are wrongly identified as not having alcoholism. Regardless, we might also ask, with success rates at best a small fraction of the total, why risk it? Our society takes a dim view of taking chances with carcinogenic substances having a kill rate of one in one million. It seems ludicrous that we do so with a substance that adversely affects the lives of 95 or 99 in 100 cases of those addicted, and many multiples of the number of addicts when we count those with whom the alcoholic comes into contact over a lifetime of drinking.

## Myth #40 (a "half-truth")
## "I can control my drinking; therefore, she should be able to do so."

Ironically, she can, and does. The alcoholic often exercises such self-restraint for decades. Richard Burton never drank during a movie production, even if he killed himself drinking. Audrey Kishline controlled her use for six years before she lost control and, at a BAL of .28 per cent, killed two innocents.

The drinking is not out of control in the early stages of alcoholism. Instead, the behaviors are—some of the time. Only in the very last stages of the disease does the alcoholic need to drink almost every waking moment.

But the close observer making this statement is not even referring to the drinking. Do we *really* care how much someone drinks if she's not bothering anyone? We rightly object to the behaviors in which those who drink heavily often engage. We might have greater success in treating alcoholism if we focus our objections on such behaviors rather than the use.

This is not to suggest that there are many heavy drinkers over 30 who are not alcoholics. These are few and far between, as are 75-year old alcoholics who don't drink before 5pm. You won't learn about these rare cases until he or she is dead, when the surviving spouse, with the right set of questions, *might* admit to having been an enabler during the entire 50 years of marriage.

# Myth #41
## "He can't control his drinking."

Consider that if a 200-pound alcoholic increases his consumption by much more than one ounce of 80-proof liquor per hour, his BAL will continue to rise. To maintain a given BAL, extraordinary self-control is necessary. As described above, early- to middle-stage alcoholics exercise such restraint every day.

Further, they go "on the wagon" for weeks or even months at a time. Actor Anthony Hopkins often took six-week breaks from drinking before he got sober. As mentioned, Richard Burton reportedly never drank during a movie production. Most alcoholics in the early-to-middle stages of their disease do not drink during the workday, and often drink only on weekends. This demonstrates extraordinary control over drinking, particularly when we consider that environmental stresses are generally greater while working than during holidays or in retirement.

# Myth #42
## "Alcoholics lack willpower."

Alcoholics often find an approximate blood alcohol level at which they function well. A 120-pound person requires the equivalent of almost 11 ounces (about one-third of a bottle) of wine *per hour* over four hours to reach a BAL of .20 per cent. Once at that level, she needs a fraction of that, only 2.5 ounces of wine per hour (or its equivalent) to *maintain* that BAL. Anyone who can reduce the drinking to that extent when already stoned has *tremendous* willpower. Yet, many early- to middle-stage alcoholics exercise such self-control for decades.

Even the latter-stage alcoholic or chronologically younger polydrug addict has far greater willpower than most non-alcoholics could ever muster. Nothing will stop him from obtaining his drug as long as he wants it.

Recall that most alcoholics are incapable of self-diagnosis until they are ready to bottom, which is a rare event in the life of an addicted person. They don't see their drinking as a problem. Therefore, it cannot be said that alcoholics do not lack willpower just because they don't want to quit. The fact that they may promise to stop is irrelevant. Such statements are meant merely to placate the few people who've forged a link between bad behaviors and heavy drinking. Alcoholics usually intend to continue drinking until well after hitting what may appear to the casual observer to be bottom after bottom. That is why close persons often wonder, hasn't he bottomed yet? Wasn't that enough pain? Due to distorted perceptions, pain that would be experienced as excruciating by the non-addicted may be barely perceptible to the alcoholic. The equivalent of a broken arm may feel only like a pinprick.

If he is allowed to continue to inflate his ego, the early-stage alcoholic may perceive such wielding of power of greater value than the loss of a limb or worse. Further, he didn't cause whatever loss occurred; others did. Therefore, the alcohol is not to blame. With this mind-set, willpower is irrelevant.

On the other hand, the latter-stage alcoholic needs the continuous flow of the drug to make up for his brain's inability to produce neurotransmitters. The pain from such loss is agonizing. We can see the results of this in the junkie's desperate attempts to obtain drugs at any price and in the alcoholic's hiding of his drug in places the rest of us would never dream. It could be argued that the fact that he pays an extraordinary price in using demonstrates amazing willpower, not a lack of it.

# Myth #43
## "He never looks drunk —
## so he can't be an alcoholic!"

Many alcoholics go through entire drinking careers without any-one realizing they've been drunk the whole time. When no longer drinking, co-workers have been known to exclaim, "I never knew you were an alcoholic until you came into work sober."

Because some alcoholics never drink during work and most don't do so for decades, many are not suspected even when in the public limelight. The case of television anchorman and rov-ing journalist George Watson is one tragic example.[60] From the age of 15 he drank heavily, usually vodka by himself late at night. Becoming an on-air fixture in the San Francisco Bay area during the 1970s and '80s, he earned over $100,000 per year, anchored the weekend news and won four Emmys for report-ing. After spending 28 days at the Betty Ford Center in early 1993, Watson let the entire Bay area know he had gotten help. Not even station KTVU general manager Kevin O'Brien had a clue that he had begun drinking again within 45 minutes of leaving the Center, having relapsed before making his announcement. He reportedly never drank during the day until sometime after this, so there weren't any physical signs that viewers or co-workers could observe. However, when Watson began daytime drinking O'Brien still didn't recognize that he was drunk, even if some of the more knowledgeable viewers may have.

Watson's four wives no doubt experienced poor behaviors spawned by an alcoholically damaged brain. His best friend and partner on most on-air assignments was cameraman Don McCauig. Finally giving up on Watson only after the latter was fired sometime after his divorce from wife number four, McCauig was stunned when Watson told him that his best friend was a bottle of vodka. More aware observers might have suspected that this could be the case sometime between wives two and three. However, such observers couldn't have guessed it by looking at his face.

# Myth #44
## "I never see her gulp, so she can't be an alcoholic."

If you see a person gulp, there is probably alcoholism. However, if the person knows to hide heavy drinking lest others become suspicious, those others will never see gulping. All anyone else will see is maintenance drinking, which as previously described ("Two or three drinks per hour are needed to maintain a given BAL"), does not look like alcoholism. And if the behaviors fail to rouse suspicions, no one will be the wiser.

# Myth #45
## "He drinks by himself, so he must be an alcoholic."

"Do you drink alone?" is one of AA's 20 questions for the possible alcoholic to ask of himself. While objective, it's worthless without adding, "often and a lot?" Even if we added this phrase, many alcoholics will respond, "What, me drink alone? That would mean I'm an alcoholic. I'm no alcoholic!" There are often so many drinking buddies that they never have to drink alone.

Few observers are privy to the information that someone drinks alone, often and a lot. On the other side of the coin, some non-alcoholics drink alone every day — a drink, or maybe two.

# Myth #46
## "One who drinks every day,
## or a lot, *must* be an alcoholic!"

A couple of drinks over the course of three-hours will result in a BAL of barely over .01 per cent for a 120-pound person and near zero for anyone over 180 pounds. One bottle of wine sipped evenly over the course of 12 hours, common among Southern Europeans, results in a BAL of essentially zero for anyone over 120 pounds. Two bottles drunk over the same period results in a BAL of .06 per cent for a 200-pound person, as does one bottle over four hours. A half bottle in two hours will do the same for a person weighing 120 pounds. This is not alcoholism.

On the other hand, two bottles over 12 hours causes the BAL to rise to .18 per cent for a 120-pound person, the same as three bottles for a 200-pounder. Again, the question must be asked: what is the weight of the drinker, how much alcohol is he consuming and over what time frame?

## Myth #47 (a "half-truth")
## "The trouble is, some people drink too much."

When we complain about someone's drinking, we really decry the resulting behaviors. Fixating on the drinking leads to serious errors in understanding and properly dealing with alcoholism.

This focus may have led Audrey Kishline into believing that her goal should be to moderate her drinking. Failing to accept or understand that biochemistry impelled her to drink excessively allowed her to believe she could continuously achieve this objective. She quotes a purported "authority" in the field, Dr. Jeffrey Schaler, who said, "Smoking cigarettes and drinking alcohol are behaviors that can lead to the diseases we call cancer of the lungs and cirrhosis of the liver. Smoking and drinking are behaviors. Cancer and cirrhosis are diseases."[61]

However the behavior is neither the problem nor the disease. Heavy drinking is a symptom of alcoholism. By obsessing over consumption, we leave open the idea that willpower can overcome a "drinking problem," making social drinking possible. If instead we hypothesize that the trouble is caused by a special biochemical processing of the drug resulting in destructive behaviors some of the time, we can eliminate any argument or hope that alcoholics need only exercise free will to control use. The problem isn't that some drink too much. The trouble arises from the fact that drinking a little sometimes impels certain people to drink more, which can cause brain damage resulting in misbehaviors in susceptible individuals.

# 4

# Beauty, Brains & Success

**Myth #48**
**"He can't be an alcoholic — he's getting**
**straight A's and, besides, he's too young."**

In her junior year in high school, Martha Morrison got straight A's and was active in the pep squad, drama club and school newspaper. During her senior year in high school, her father "knew something was wrong with her," but didn't know what. She was misdiagnosed as paranoid-schizophrenic soon after. During college, she told her parents she'd earn straight A's. She kept her promise, went on to medical school, received almost all honors during her last two years and passed all of her licensing exams "with flying colors." As a psychiatric resident, she counseled drug addicts for two years. Yet, from junior high through high school, college and medical school, Martha Morrison was addicted to an enormous array of psychotropic drugs.[63]

She became a full-blown Darvon addict at age 12 and an alcoholic by the time she was 13. At 17, Morrison was using methamphetamines daily, along with "astonishing" amounts of non-prescription stimulants and prescription drugs like Vivarin, Nodoz, Robitussin and Romilar with codeine. She often used mescaline, psilocybin, THC, PCP, Darvon, marijuana and LSD. Late in her medical residency program at age 29, when a psychiatrist friend misdiagnosed her as having Bipolar Disorder, she was regularly ingesting Demerol, Mepergan, cocaine and other stimulants, Tenuate, Ritalin, Fastin, Valium, Ativan, Serax, Percodan, Cogentin, Artane, marijuana, alcohol, codeine, Tylox and Demerol.[64]

Actress Drew Barrymore tells us she drank addictively at age 8. There are few ages at which one is "too young" to be alcoholic. Because the addict needs to inflate the ego and one way to do this is to excel, school (and later work) is usually the last endeavor at which the addict will fail. This is the reason some addicts achieve straight A's in school, get promotions at work, perform magnificently for the camera and fans, build business empires and compose or write extraordinary works, while they ruin relationships, betray friends, lie to family members and destroy lives.

## Myth #49
## "She's too successful to be an alcoholic."

Let's see. We'll try with just a few names to disavow the reader of the idea that anyone can be too successful or wealthy to have alcoholism.

From professional sports: Ty Cobb, Mickey Mantle, Babe Ruth, Darryl Strawberry, Dennis Rodman, Chris Webber (NBA), Ken Daneyko (NHL), Daron Oshay "Mookie" Blaylock (NBA) and Johnny Tapia (five-time world boxing champion in three different weight divisions).

From the big screen: Vivien Leigh, Marilyn Monroe, Tony Curtis, Peter Lawford and Frank Sinatra (who once "went on a three-day Jack Daniels binge and totally destroyed his office at" his home).[65] Elizabeth Taylor, Richard Burton, Robert Downey, Jr., Robin Williams, Tim Allen, Tobey Maguire, Dick Van Dyke, Mary Tyler Moore, Paula Poundstone, Christian Slater, Richard Dreyfus and Keanu Reeves (in my opinion shows indications of alcoholism). Nick Nolte, George C. Scott, Tom Sizemore (in my opinion shows indications of alcoholism — domestic abuse committed when drunk against ex-wife actress/tennis player Maeve Quinlan and, later, ex-fiance Heidi Fleiss).[66] John Belushi, Chris Farley, Bette Davis, Joan Crawford, Anthony

Hopkins, Samuel L. Jackson, Jason Robards, John Spencer ("The West Wing") and Anthony Michael Hall (member of the Hollywood "Brat Pack").[67]

Politicians and other government officials: Huey Long, Wilbur Mills and John Tower (Republican Senator from Texas, rejected as George Bush Sr.'s choice for secretary of defense largely because of what had by then become obvious alcoholism).[68] Joseph McCarthy (Republican Senator who led the charge in making mostly false accusations of communist affiliations in the early 1950s), Ted Kennedy and Supreme Court Chief Justice William O. Douglas. Their behaviors and actions suggest that Presidents Andrew Johnson (who was impeached by Congress and acquitted by a single vote), Lyndon Johnson and John Kennedy (possible polydrug addict) were alcoholics. Bill Clinton's adolescent-like misbehaviors are strongly suggestive of alcoholism. President George W. Bush has been a recovering alcoholic since age 40.

An estimated 20% of doctors and attorneys. This includes Roy Cohn, one of the toughest and most brilliant lawyers ever, who was disbarred just before his death in 1986.

From the boardroom: Henry Ford ll, Ted Turner, and probably many of those involved in the corporate scandals of the late 1990s and early 2000s.

Award-winning film makers: Oliver Stone (arrested for suspicion of DUI and possession of hashish, June 11, 1999,The Los Angeles Daily News, "Stone jailed; no conspiracy cited," June 12, 1999.The Los Angeles Daily News, "Stone jailed; no conspiracy cited," June 12, 1999.[69] Aaron Sorkin (creator and Executive Producer, "West Wing"), Sam Peckinpah and Don Simpson (Jerry Bruckheimer's partner in producing such hits as "Beverly Hills Cop" and "Top Gun," whose body was found "loaded with a combination of prescription and nonprescription medications").[70]

Musicians: Elvis Presley, John Lennon and Chuck Negron (Three Dog Night singer, who "despite" selling 50 million albums was a slave to heroin for 23 years.)[71] Jim Morrison (Doors), Janis Joplin, Brian Jones (Rolling Stones), Syd Barrett (Pink Floyd), Keith Moon (The Who), David Crosby, Brian

Wilson (Beach Boys), Glenn Campbell, Sade, Mary J. Blige and Rob Pilatos (Milli Vanilli). Miles Davis, Marvin Gaye, Earle "Bud" Powell, John Coltrane, Leon "Bix" Beiderbecke, Sheila Jordan, Billie Holiday, Art Pepper, Hank Williams, Paul Williams (The Temptations) and Charlie Parker. Beethoven, Mozart, Bradley Nowell (Sublime), Kurt Cobain (Nirvana), Sid Vicious (Sex Pistols), A.J. McLean (Backstreet Boys), Scott Weiland (Stone Temple Pilots), Steven Tyler (Aerosmith) and Layne Staley (Alice in Chains). James Hetfield and probably the entire Metallica band, commercially the greatest heavy-metal success in history, referred to by fans as Alcoholica.[72] Music producer Phil Spector.

In fact, alcoholism seems to *increase* the odds of over-achievement in occupations that allow the exercise of power over fans, constituents, customers, patients and employees. An estimated 33% of Academy Award® winning best actors and 26% of winning best actresses have been alcoholics.[73] Many top executives have alcoholism. The best estimates as to the number of alcoholic doctors, attorneys and politicians suggest a far higher incidence than in the overall population. Alcoholism among professional athletes is epidemic, including some of the greatest sports stars of all time. Research by a University of Calgary economist, Christopher Auld, found that teetotalers earn 10% less than moderate and heavy drinkers. He notes that the "alcohol-income puzzle" has been "well-known amongst economists for a decade," and that he is only confirming earlier research.[74] When we understand the role of alcohol in causing the predisposed to have a need to wield power over others, this finding makes sense, even if the implications are repugnant.

# Myth #50
## "She's too smart to be an alcoholic."

Martha Morrison's story proves that extraordinary intelligence is no impediment to alcoholism. In fact, many believe that the average alcoholic has *higher* innate intelligence than does the typical non-alcoholic. Future studies, however, may show that *developed* intelligence is connected to alcoholism, due to the drive in the early-stage alcoholic to overachieve. This propensity may explain why there is no shortage of very bright addicts. Donald Goodwin, M.D., identified five of eight Nobel Prize winning authors from the United States during the 20th century as alcoholics: William Faulkner, Ernest Hemingway, Sinclair Lewis, Eugene O'Neill and John Steinbeck.[75]

Alcoholism also appears to be an equal-opportunity disease regardless of political persuasion. Existentialist Marxist philosopher Jean-Paul Sartre was an alcoholic,[76] as have likely been many other totalitarian socialists and fascists. One could speculate that this may be due to the fact that the alcoholic compulsion to wield power is most effectively achieved via a totalitarian state, even if vicarious. On the other side of the political spectrum, three of my favorite philosophers and political thinkers were addicts. The great philosopher-revolutionary Thomas Paine had alcoholism, while philosopher and author Herbert Spencer was addicted to laudanum (a mixture of alcohol and morphine popular in the 1800s) and Ayn Rand, to amphetamines. The latter controlled her followers by allowing no deviation or room for argument, becoming a cult-like figure in the process. She also exercised power over her husband and a younger surrogate by engaging in a bizarre open affair for decades. Even though well hidden or ignored because no one before suspected or had a clue as to its significance, future alco-historians will likely find alcohol or other drug addiction in many great scientists and brilliant philosophers.

## Myth #51
## "He's too charming to be an alcoholic!"

One might think that alcoholism and charm don't mix. When we envision the late-stage alcoholic vomiting in his own bed, charm is the last thing that comes to mind.

However, early-stage alcoholism looks very different from the latter-stage version. Due to the addict's need to inflate his ego, over-achievement and success often mark the early stages.

Because seductive appeal can be used to get one's way, too much of it can be a sign of alcoholism.

An estimated 80 to 90% of incarcerated prisoners have alcoholism. There's no reason to believe that the rate varies by crime, or might be any different among those who aren't, but should be, in prison. Con men, engaging in the non-violent crime of persuading others that lies are truths, should end up in prison even if they don't. The primary means by which they achieve their criminal aims is by charming the victim. As is true for other crooks, the majority of such charmers may be alcoholics. It is not necessarily the end result of theft that excites them, so much as the power-game of the process and their own brilliance, even if the financial gain yields power as well. However, there are large gaps in the histories of famous con men. As previously mentioned, biographers generally don't know that heavy use of alcohol is relevant to understanding their subjects. Even if they do, they may not have access to accurate information on actual use.

Charles Ponzi was one of these subjects. The idea behind his crime, which continues today in various forms under the label "Ponzi scheme," is to pay exceptionally high returns on investments by covertly using funds from new investors to pay previous ones. The swindle is uncovered sooner or later, when it collapses from a dearth of new investors while the perpetrator disappears in Rio de Janeiro.

Ponzi's biographer Donald H. Dunn mentions Ponzi's drinking only three times over a span of 254 pages. The reader is told at the outset that the events recorded were as factually true as Dunn's extensive research could make them and that "although treated novelistically, *what* happens is grounded thoroughly in reality."[77] He tells of Ponzi drinking white wine "quickly in several gulps" and of needing pills for a sour stomach because he had "too much wine today."[78] Heavy drinking despite physical discomfort so severe that a biographer would mention it is a subtle indicator of alcoholism. Ponzi also added a "heavy splash of anisette to his fourth cup of coffee," and ended the day with "a large meal and innumerable glasses of fine French wine."[79] Long after the fraud was exposed, Ponzi was divorced, released from prison and deported to Italy. His high-ranking Italian friends put out enough cash "for the aging swindler to get drunk frequently and gamble...in a neighborhood bar."[80] This was the extent of Dunn's remarks on Ponzi's drinking. Considering the fact that Dunn had no idea it was even relevant, the likelihood of alcoholism being the motive force behind his need to con others is high, especially since Ponzi appears to have eventually succumbed to latter-stage alcoholism.

It also appears that many serial murderers have used charm to lure their victims into harm's way. Anyone who can entice teenagers into his home at the first meeting, as did alcoholic John Wayne Gacy, **must** be charming. According to James Graham, Gacy was "active in local politics, the church and the Junior Chamber of Commerce. He performed as a volunteer clown at hospitals, and once had his picture taken with the First Lady, Rosalyn Carter." He tricked young boys into being handcuffed, after which he raped, tortured and murdered them.[81] Likewise, alcoholic Ted Bundy, who bedded and then murdered at least 21 women, must have had extraordinary charm. Charm, like intimidation, is merely another tool by which the addict achieves his goal of wielding capricious power over others. And, no one is more charming than is a practicing alcoholic who chooses this method.

## Myth #52
## "One who never misses a day of work and is rarely late couldn't be an alcoholic."

Grace Slick, lead singer for the Jefferson Airplane, was known for her reliability. She always arrived early for appointments and, as a periodic drinker, mostly drank on her nights off. While many rock stars were high during most concerts, she was noticeably drunk on stage probably only ten times. The fact that she blew only a few concerts was a remarkable feat in an occupational setting that condoned almost anything in the drugged-out late '60s and '70s.[82]

One would imagine that in a more conservative environment, she might never have shown up to work high and would have been even more reliable. Indeed, many recovering addicts report that however bad their off-work behaviors may have been, they rarely if ever missed work and never showed up late.

# Myth #53
## "He can't be an alcoholic because I've never seen him with red eyes."

Red eyes affect only a select few and even then, only when on certain drugs. Many addicts' eyes never turn red, while the eyes of some non-addicts do so with a blood alcohol level as low as .04 per cent. More likely, the eyes may appear glassy, as did Marilyn Monroe's in her later films. Younger addicts may seem sensuous with a "bedroom eyes" look, while the eyes of older addicts may appear tired even if glassy, as did Henri Paul's in the hotel video prior to the tragedy in which he killed himself and Princess Diana. Those using marijuana often have glassy, red eyes, while stimulants can result in a glazed or tired look due to lack of sleep.

Pupil size gives away far more. When the dark area of the eye is less than a fifth in diameter of the iris, opiate use is indicated. This includes addictive use of the legal drugs Oxycontin and Vicodin as well as heroin. In adults, pupils slightly over half the size of the iris in the light signal heavy alcohol or marijuana use. Anything larger is an almost certain sign of non-caffeine stimulants in non-therapeutic doses. However, highly tolerant users may display these symptoms for only a short period after snorting or injecting. Since the addict knows his eyes can give away his secret, he is usually careful to hide them behind sun glasses even in dark rooms or not appear in public until the eyes look normal. Actor Jack Nicholson may be an example of one who cares about his image. On the other hand,

Palestinian authority president Yasser Arafat apparently didn't care—his amphetamine-enlarged pupils, big as the moon, adorn page 43 of the September 18, 2003 issue of "The Economist" magazine.

## Myth #54
### "She can't be an alcoholic—look at what great shape she's in."

Professional ice skater Tanya Harding was arrested for driving under the influence—DUI—at age 31 with a .16 per cent BAL, which is in itself a compelling indication of alcoholism.[83] Baseball greats Darryl Strawberry and Steve Howe are known addicts, as were Ty Cobb and Mickey Mantle. Martial arts actor Jean-Claude Van Damme, arrested at age 38 on suspicion of DUI,[84] had previously checked himself into drug rehab in 1996 and then stopped using "cold turkey" two years later.[85] Former British Open and PGA champion John Daly trashed a hotel room in a drunken rage in March 1997.[86] New York Giants quarterback Kerry Collins is a known addict, as are numerous other professional football players.

A study reported by Harvard's School of Public Health found that college athletes often binge-drink more than non-athletes.[87] Binge drinking is an indication of alcoholism. Many alcoholics are in great shape—in the early stages of their disease.

## Myth #55
### "Someone who has everything, including great looks, couldn't possibly be an alcoholic."

Elizabeth Taylor, Baywatch beauty Yasmine Bleeth and Shannen Doherty, a star on TV's "Beverly Hills 90210" and "Charmed" who was arrested on suspicion of DUI December 28, 2000,[88] are gorgeous addicts. So was Marilyn Monroe who, as a result of "habitual tardiness and absenteeism, difficulty in remembering lines, and conflicts with most of her co-workers" while starring in Billy Wilder's "Some Like It Hot," made life miserable for co-workers.[89] Yancy Butler, the sultry star of TV's "Witchblade," checked herself into rehab in June 2002. Nerine Shatner, former runner-up in the Miss World competition and late wife of actor William Shatner showed signs of alcoholism. Susan Hayward, Jean Harlow, Vivien Leigh and Natalie Wood were all likely alcoholics.[90] Diana Ross, the former Supremes singer, was admitted into rehab in 2002. Marion Davies, William Randolph Hearst's long-time mistress, was a known alcoholic. Demi Moore, Dennis Quaid and Don Johnson all show indications of alcoholism.[91] Jamie Lee Curtis and Charlie Sheen admit to being in recovery. Having everything including terrific looks does not inoculate against alcoholism.

## Myth #56
## "If a person at the top of his profession or social sphere were an alcoholic, the public would know!"

When employers, politicians or other top figures are identified as alcoholics, employees, spouses and close others risk the loss of prestige, position, power and income. Therefore, the higher the social, political, business or professional status of the addict the more diligently such persons strive to protect the secret.

The late Mark Hughes was such a figure. The founder and chairman of Herbalife, a major nutritional supplement company, Hughes owned a $30 million estate in Malibu, California. He was found dead from an overdose of alcohol and anti-depressants at age 44. Even after this tragedy, his staff was intent on rescuing him. When I publicly suggested that anyone at his age who drank to such excess while using anti-depressants likely suffered from alcoholism, I was lambasted by his office for "maligning" a "great man." Great and extraordinarily successful though he may have been, my intent was not to defame, but rather to educate. It was later reported that Hughes' death followed "a four-day drinking binge."[92] Many extremely successful people have untreated alcoholism, which is not to anyone's benefit when they die from their disease.

The public hasn't a clue to the number of commercial pilots with alcoholism and, because of the reputations the airlines wish to protect, such information isn't easy to come by. Therefore, it was a stroke of luck that America West pilot Thomas Cloyd, 44, and copilot Christopher Hughes, 41, were stopped by an airport screener as they attempted to pass through a checkpoint with coffee in hand. Only when an argument ensued over bringing in the coffee did the screener notice that both were bleary-eyed and reeked of alcohol. They tested at over twice the federal legal limit for operating a motor vehicle. Considering that most early-stage alcoholics do not show up to work drunk, the fact that there were even nine alcohol violations among 10,000 pilots and flight attendants tested by the FAA in 2001 is alarming. More frightening is that, according to police reports, Cloyd was in a "drunken fracas with his wife, spit on her, cursed at her and shoved her against a refrigerator" a few years earlier. "'When Tom's drinking,' [his wife] told cops, 'it doesn't take anything to start him fighting.'"[93]

We might think that the public would be aware of alcoholism in someone as important to the lives of others as pilots long before reaching the point at which they show up to work drunk. If there are obvious indications of alcoholism elsewhere in the life of a pilot, as was the case for Thomas Cloyd, he should be offered a choice of sobriety or loss of flight privileges. Cloyd's wife, like spouses, employees and others close to millions of alcoholics, likely felt she had too much to lose by outing her husband. Friends and law enforcers also probably figured it wasn't their business to interfere in his work, regardless of private events. Yet, if we are to prevent tragedy, alcoholism needs to become *everyone's* business.

If the public knew to look for the telltale ego-inflating behavioral indications of alcoholism, they would get suspicious even in the absence of blatantly obvious poor behaviors. However, the public isn't aware of the subtle behavioral indications such as the pious and arrogant attitude displayed by

Rush Limbaugh prior to his visit to rehab. More obvious clues, unless criminal, are not usually widely disseminated, or are considered tabloid-like rumors and not taken seriously. Therefore, the public is often the *last* to know that a well-known, successful person has alcoholism.

## Myth #57
## "A person at the top of her profession or social sphere is not likely to remain an alcoholic for very long, because her money will save her. After all, she has access to the best medical care that money can buy."

Mark Hughes was a mega-millionaire. The problem was not that he couldn't afford excellent medical care; the trouble was that he, like millions of other alcoholics, didn't want anything to interfere with his excessive drinking. The same could be said for multi-millionaire Rush Limbaugh and his addiction to hero-in-like prescription drugs. In most cases, one of lower status attempting to meddle would be summarily fired or otherwise eliminated from his life.

Close persons, trying to preserve their own positions, often guard the alcoholic from consequences of misbehaviors. The loftier the office, the greater the protection. Therefore, the higher the social, political, business or professional status of the addict, the greater the enabling. Thus, wealth *prevents* many alcoholics from getting sober.

Addiction experts have long observed that given two alcoholics, one with money and the other without but otherwise equal, the latter stands a greater chance of becoming sober and staying that way. Money is an enormous obstacle to sobriety. It's a good thing that attending 90 AA meetings in 90 days for $90 in voluntary donations is affordable even for the addict who has lost virtually everything.

# Myth #58
## "He can be reasoned with; after all, he's an intelligent human being."

Alcoholism damages the neo-cortex, the human part of the brain responsible for reason and logic. Because the lower brain centers are fixed at birth, they cannot be damaged. It's folly to try reasoning with a damaged neo-cortex and a fully functional reptilian brain, the sole purpose of which is to insure base survival.

Yet, we often attempt to reason with such people. When this occurs, we should stand back and ask, "Am I frustrated because I am trying to be logical with a person who cannot think rationally, because he or she may have a damaged brain?" If this is even a remote possibility, we should assume alcoholism. By doing so, we will not only often find alcoholism where never suspected, but also preserve our sanity.

# Myth #59
## "Psychological problems stemming from being the child of an alcoholic best explain adolescent-like behaviors in highly intelligent and successful people."

While they *could* explain such behaviors, they usually do not *best* explain them. We couldn't do better in considering this idea than by analyzing the greatest example ever of an extraordinarily gifted person engaging in an amazing array of otherwise inexplicable behaviors: former President Bill Clinton.

No pundit's attempted psychoanalysis of Clinton's adolescent-like misbehaviors while in office considered the possibility of alcoholism. Instead the public was led to believe that Clinton, a highly intelligent man, was just stupid in his private behavior. While possible, this is unlikely. Further, he allegedly raped Juanita Broderick years earlier, a claim for which the circumstantial evidence is excellent. The odds that a person committing a rape is alcoholic are in the neighborhood of 80 to 90%.

73

In his last act as President, Clinton pardoned over 150 hardened criminals. This action was one of the most extraordinary public displays ever of an alcoholic sense of invincibility, in which the adolescent mind-set says, "Watch me, watch what I can get away with." What better way for the addict to inflate his ego than by thumbing his nose at everyone around him, in this case an entire country?

In-between these acts, Clinton engaged in a tremendous amount of sexually compulsive behavior, which alone is enough to ascribe a 50% likelihood of alcoholism. At least one sexual incident strongly suggesting it wasn't "just sex" was the groping of Kathleen Wiley in the Oval Office in the middle of the afternoon. It may be suggested that no man would grope a woman in the way and under the circumstances described unless he's high as a kite. Anyone that loaded in the middle of the day has a very high probability of having alcoholism, regardless of the office he holds. Governor Arnold Schwarzenegger's inappropriate groping of women on Hollywood movie sets can be ascribed to having been a child of an alcoholic. Wiley, on the other hand, was asking Clinton for help in dealing with an extraordinarily difficult personal problem, one so disturbing that her husband was reported to have committed suicide at almost the same moment. The circumstances of the groping were as different as night and day.

I once called radio talk-show host Larry Elder, who is no fan of Bill Clinton, when another caller lambasted George W. Bush for being an alcoholic and allegedly having used cocaine. I explained that Bush is a recovering alcoholic, sober since age 40 and, in my opinion showing excellent recovery considering the challenging circumstances of his presidency. I suggested, on the other hand, that the President before him exhibited numerous behavioral indications of active alcoholism, which is of great concern when the alcoholic has enormous power. Elder said that on his show I could call Clinton a sex addict, but not an alcoholic. I told him the odds that sexually compulsive behaviors were rooted in alcoholism are 50%. As I attempted to explain the need for alcoholics to wield power, forging the link between this and serial Don Juanism, Larry responded, "We're not going there on this show" and hung up.

The implication in his reluctance to "go there," is that identifying the possibility of alcoholism is an accusation worse than calling someone a liar, womanizer and adulterer, which Elder readily admits is true of Bill Clinton. As repeatedly stated, alcoholism is a biological flaw that causes serious personality defects and results in observably destructive behaviors. It's a shame that Elder, who I view as a brilliantly astute political observer, doesn't seem to understand alcoholism. Let's once and for all give Bill Clinton the benefit of the doubt. In the same way that I view the idiotic private behaviors of my favorite philosophers (Paine, Spencer and Rand) to addiction, we should assume that Clinton's inane adolescent sexual compulsions, along with much of his other behaviors, were rooted in alcoholism. If we don't assume this, we're left with the idea that he never mustered the intellectual capacity to grow up emotionally despite not inheriting alcoholism from his more obvious alcoholic parents. If he is as intelligent as he has been given credit, this possibility should be considered remote.

"I never knew a person become insane who was not in the habit of taking a portion of alcohol daily."
— Benjamin Parsons, English clergyman, 1840[94]

# 5

# Abuse & Dysfunction

**Myth #60**
**"Most misbehaviors can't be attributed**
**to alcoholism. Those who engage in such**
**behaviors are usually fundamentally**
**bad people and *not* alcoholic."**

Although it may be comforting to believe this, the facts don't support the assertion. There is no difference in aggregate levels of misbehaviors and psychopathologies in children who later trigger alcoholism vs. those who are not alcoholics. In sobriety, alcoholics are almost always non-destructive, productive people. Serially poor behaviors are rarely found in non-alcoholics. Therefore, we should assume alcoholism is at the root of any serious or serial misbehavior.

The fact that terrible behaviors rarely occur in non-alcoholics suggests that the most horrific serial and mass murderers may have been alcohol or other drug addicts. The fact is, most of them are. This includes Charles Manson, John Wayne Gacy, Ted Bundy, Jeffrey Dahmer, Jeremy Strohmeyer, Eric Harris and most of the other monsters in history. This doesn't mean that we should forgive the behaviors or fail to impose consequences. However, it does suggest that we re-think the death penalty. By coercing abstinence and rewarding sobriety among inmates, we might dramatically increase the numbers of those who find redemption. More important, if we act early, quickly and decisively in stopping the progression of the disease in those who have not yet acted criminally, there might be fewer alcoholics committing heinous crimes.

I didn't begin my research on alcoholism with a preconceived notion that most people are fundamentally good. It might be taken as a measure of faith to believe that they are. However, we don't need to rely on unproven assertions. By studying recovering alcoholics and alcoholism, we find they usually *are* decent and were turned into monsters as a result of brain damage rooted in alcoholic biochemistry. As James Graham points out, even a Ted Bundy might not have murdered anyone had he been "diagnosed and successfully treated for [alcoholism] at an early age."[95]

# Myth #61
## "Being a great liar doesn't make a person an alcoholic."

Recovering alcoholics must become very honest if they are to remain sober. This is especially true among themselves, at AA meetings, where those with whom they share their secrets more easily understand and forgive. A refrain often heard at such meetings is, "When we drank, we lied, cheated, stole and manipulated. When we used, we could not be trusted." They admit to being the world's greatest liars when drinking.

There are three main reasons that account for this. The first is that there is no sneakier way by which to control others. There are several ways of wielding such power. One of the most destructive is by making false accusations, particularly within the criminal justice system. The results of such lies were devastating for the victims in a spate of trials in the late 20th century alleging child abuse. Most of these turned out to be witch-hunts, tragically destroying the lives of entire families. The original accusation of the commission of horrifying abuse made against several members of the Buckey family, who operated the McMartin Pre-School in Manhattan Beach, California, was made by an addict, Judy Johnson. Alcohol, and therefore alcoholics (bad behavior was connected to the use of the drug), fuelled the Salem Witch-Hunts. False accusations of adultery made by the addict who herself commits the act is, according to many recovering addicts, almost as common as the adultery itself in which addicts frequently engage. Both false accusations and adultery, along with Don Juanism, require a series of carefully planned lies and deceit. In other instances, alcoholics lie only to prove what they can get away with, often in an attempt to make others think highly of them for spurious achievements and prowess—a more subtle form of control.

The second reason addicts become great liars is to protect either their source of drugs, which is common among illegal drug addicts, or the fact that they are using at all, routine with latter-stage alcoholics. Sometimes, successful hiding occurs over many years. Alcoholism with its bad behaviors can lay low for years, while the alcoholic slowly ups the intake and, perhaps, adds a drug here and a drug there with a doctor's script. More than once, Vicodin and other legal pharmaceuticals have been discovered buried in a drawer by a spouse, for whom the gradually increasing verbal abuse over decades of marriage suddenly made sense.

Third, an appearance of lying results from the fact that the addict may, quite simply, not remember the truth. This occurs most often in convincing fashion due to euphoric recall, in which everything is remembered in a self-favoring light. Along with blackouts and memory repression, this distortion gives an *appearance* of lying. As observers, we may be unable to determine the basis for lies. As the lying proliferates, regardless of reason, the odds of addiction increase.

There are so many ways and reasons for the addict to lie that untruths become pervasive. Applying a little probability to this is not dissimilar to analyzing why the odds are high that someone committing a traffic infraction is DUI and, therefore, a likely alcoholic. For example, alcoholics engage in illegal U-turns so much more frequently than do non-alcoholics that the odds of someone engaging in such an act being under the influence is 35%, even though on average only two per cent of all drivers are high. The same idea can be applied to lying. Even the most scrupulous may exaggerate or inadvertently tell a little white lie from time to time; however, alcoholics do so far more often. Therefore, the odds that someone lying is alcoholic are greater than we might otherwise think, especially if he wields power by becoming a *great* liar and in turn uses this ability to further such power.

The labels of various psychotropic drugs prescribed by doctors include warnings of impaired speech and memory, paranoia, drowsiness and mental confusion. Labels on alcohol warn that consumption impairs the ability to drive a car or operate machinery, drinking may cause health problems and women should not drink during pregnancy because of the risk of birth defects. These warnings in a more enlightened society might include an increased probability of lying.

## Myth #62
## "She just has a insatiable need to win."

At the end of the posthumous biography of her mother, actress Bette Davis, B. D. Hyman shares that what she didn't understand "was that fighting is done for its own sake, not just to win an *argument*, but to prove who's *strong* enough to win."[96] Hyman missed the source of this insatiable need, explaining that the heavy drinking was, along with all her other character flaws, one of its results. As is typical in trying to excuse alcoholism, she reversed cause and effect.

Hyman describes alcoholic behavior after behavior in her famous mother throughout the 282 pages of text.[97] After mentioning drinking and pharmaceutical drug use only a few times, she finally points to alcoholism on page 269, with Davis in the hospital after suffering a series of strokes. Her lifelong physician, Vincent Carroll, was agitated over the fact that Davis was exhibiting signs of alcoholic withdrawal, apparently undiagnosed by the attending physicians. [98] He knew that such withdrawal can be life threatening if untreated.

This need explains why so many successful entrepreneurs, athletes, celebrities and politicians are alcoholics. They do not become alcoholics as a result of stardom but rather become stars because of their alcoholism. The same chemical buildup of poison on the brain that results in destructive behaviors is often at the root of constructive ones, including becoming the best at something. He who is best wields enormous power and influence over fans, customers, patients, clients and constituents, serving to feed the alcoholic ego.

Non-alcoholics do sometimes have an insatiable need to win. However, the more that need comes at any cost, the greater the likelihood of alcoholism as the motive force behind it.


# Myth #63
## "His real personality comes out when he drinks."

This is one of the most pervasive and destructive myths, when applied to alcoholics.

The *real* personality of the alcoholic eventually emerges well after his last drink, usually five or ten years later. The personality manifesting during a period of active alcoholism is a toxic one and is as opposite of "real" as we'll ever see.

The poisonous buildup of acetaldehyde occurring in alcoholics results in damage to the human part of the brain, the neo-cortex, allowing the reptilian brain, the basal ganglia, to override rational restraints. Since the basal ganglia is the part of the brain responsible for pre-mammalian instincts, impulses and survival, pre-civilized behavior results. This is not the real human being.

Most alcoholics exhibit an array of personality disorders, loosely called "personality defects" by members of Alcoholics Anonymous. Even AA seems to imply that these defects of personality caused them to become alcoholics. As previously noted, however, the opposite is true: alcoholism causes most personality problems.

When psychological tests are administered to practicing alcoholics and recovering ones with up to 10 days sobriety, many appear to have measurable psychopathologies. The fact that when the tests are repeated after three months of sobriety 70 to 80% of these problem pathologies disappear supports the idea that the personality exhibited by practicing alcoholics is not innate. EEG brain waves and CAT scans require up to two years for normalcy to return after drinking ceases in alcoholics.[99] Damage to the neo-cortex creates the personality observed in the practicing alcoholic, resulting in a god-like sense of invincibility and inordinately large sense of self importance, or inflated ego. The *real* person, then, is Dr. Jekyll, not Mr. Hyde.

## Myth #64
## "Personality disorders are more common than alcoholism," or a variation, "He's no alcoholic—he's just crazy!"

We might, again, give people the benefit of the doubt and assume alcoholism. After all, which is worse-inheriting a biological disorder that causes what appear to be signs of insanity, or actually being insane?

Recovering alcoholics often report that their biggest enablers were therapists, who gave them all the excuses in the world to continue drinking. Ideas such as, "Your parents beat you, no wonder you drink!" or, "You grew up destitute, no wonder you use drugs!" are fed into the minds of addicts by psychologists who fail to grasp the biological roots of alcoholism. The problem is, this disease causes the afflicted to engage in behaviors that make it appear he is not sane. In other words, alcoholism mimics almost every mental disorder. The misdiagnosed run the gamut from early- to latter-stage alcohol and other drug addiction, varying tremendously in degree, generally becoming more obvious with poly-drug use or during middle-stage alcoholism and beyond.[100]

Since third-party payers often refuse to reimburse for alcohol and other drug addiction treatment, referring to inexplicable behaviors as "Personality Disorders" are the psychologists' way of making insurance companies liable. When treatment is covered, alcoholism is more frequently diagnosed. However, it may take a generation for therapists to accept the idea that few instances of Personality Disorders exist independently of addiction. There's simply too much time, effort and money invested in one's prior education. When I explained my view that because alcoholism mimics virtually all of the Disorders the underlying problem is usually alcoholism, one therapist said to me, "you're suggesting that practically everything I learned to become a therapist is worthless." There are both special interests and psychological ones working to maintain the status quo.

Yet, it should not be surprising that alcoholism takes form as one or more of these Disorders. Active addiction causes the afflicted to engage in behaviors that violate core values. The conflict between behaviors and values feeds on itself, leading to repeated violations. This subjects the person to intense stress, causing him to play "Survival Games" that look like Personality Disorders. Most alcoholics succumb to this, at least to some extent.

The Disorders that are mimicked vary by type of drug and the Psychological Type of the addict. There is also an interrelationship between an addict's Type and the drugs he chooses. In addition, the drug often acts to determine the Disorder(s) mimicked. While the details are beyond the scope of this book, an overview and one in-depth example will serve as evidence that most "crazies" are alcoholics or children of addicts who have, simply, not grown up emotionally.[101]

The main Disorders, listed in the psychologists' manual entitled, *Diagnostic and Statistical Manual of Mental Disorders, Fourth Edition*, or *DSM-IV™*, are names most lay people have heard.[102] These include Anti-Social Personality Disorder, Obsessive-Compulsive Personality Disorder, Dissociative Identity Disorder (formerly known as Multiple Personality Disorder), Borderline Personality Disorder, Schizophrenia, Paranoid Personality Disorder, Bipolar Disorder (formerly known as Manic Depressive) and Narcissistic Personality Disorder. Many therapists attempt to treat Disorders in what often turns out to be a mistaken belief that one or more of these is the source of problems, rather than alcoholism. "Dual-diagnosis," in which a patient is diagnosed with alcoholism *and* one or more of the Disorders, is all the rage even among many chemical dependency counselors. When asked how he could know whether a true Disorder exists until the alcoholism is in remission, one such counselor admitted that while he could not, insurance and government programs pay the costs of treating just about any Disorder he identifies. Another became visibly agitated when asked how symptoms could be treated without dealing with the underlying cause.

**Anti-Social Personality Disorder** requires "a pervasive pattern of disregard for and violation of the rights of others."[103] *The 16th Edition of the Merck Manual* (another important text for psychologists) describes that persons having this Disorder "flout normal rules of social order. [They] are impulsive, irresponsible, amoral, and unable to forgo immediate gratification..."[104] This "rules are not for me" attitude is one of the hallmarks of many alcoholics. The impulsive inclination and need for immediate gratification hints at damage to a neo-cortex that has allowed the impulsive and emotional areas of the brain to run free of rational restraints.

Addiction expert Terence T. Gorski administered the MMPI (the psychologists' tool for diagnosing Disorders) to a group of recovering alcoholics five days into a program of sobriety and again 20 days later. The percentage scoring as likely sociopaths plummeted from over 90% to less than 10%, providing further support for the idea that alcoholism is *usually* at the root of behaviors commonly believed to indicate the existence of Personality Disorders.[105]

Behaviors manifesting as **Bipolar Disorder**, formerly known as manic-depression, may result from extended amphetamine or cocaine use followed by a period of abstinence, or depressant drug use. Numerous therapists having an interest in historical analysis have misdiagnosed Adolf Hitler as having been Bipolar. However, he was an amphetamine addict from 1936 on, and a barbiturate user during WW-II. The grandiose scheme laid out in *Mein Kampf* indicates the possibility of barbiturate addiction long before this time, but his mood swings became far more extreme and behaviors much more erratic during the known period in which amphetamine-barbiturate use was combined.[106]

Actress Vivien Leigh was repeatedly diagnosed as bipolar even while she regularly drank heavily. Copious drinking also preceded Patty Duke's well-known Bipolar Disorder. As previously mentioned, by age 14 she was drinking Bloody Marys with her business managers. She didn't have her first bipolar episode until she was 19. The fact that in her twenties she was often "hung over most of the day because I drank most of the night," is a powerful indicator of alcoholism.[107]

Bipolar Disorder no doubt exists independently of alcoholism. However, it is frequently diagnosed either when it is a symptom or has been triggered by addiction. The same may be true for **Schizophrenia**. Perhaps the best-known Schizophrenic in recent times is mathematician John Nash, portrayed in the movie "A Beautiful Mind." The first Schizophrenic episode depicted was one in which Nash was drinking to a degree that could be considered bingeing with his imaginary friend. If true, alcoholism may have triggered or exacerbated Nash's Schizophrenia. Support for the idea that what appears to be Schizophrenia may often be rooted in alcoholism can be found in the observation that, according to author Anne Wilson Schaef, Ph.D., "when the term 'schizophrenia' was first coined, [the definition] included alcoholism."[108] In addition, the illness is usually first observed in the middle teens to late twenties, generally well after use of alcohol and other drugs has begun.[109] Alcoholism is rarely suspected, since most doctors grasp so little about it and hardly any consider the possibility at such a young age.

This is not to suggest that Schizophrenia does not exist without alcoholism. On the other hand, as early as 1897 Henry Maudley, M.D., found that "intemperance stands next to [hereditary influence] in the list of efficient causes" of insanity. Maudley based his opinion in part on the experience of an asylum for the mentally ill in the early 1870s. (Although some may consider the idea of citing a report this early in the history of behavioral science questionable, we would today be hard-pressed to repeat what amounts to an extraodinary study of the results of coerced abstinence.) During the second half of 1871, only 24 new male patients were admitted to this asylum, "whereas there were 47 and 73 in the preceding and succeeding half years. During the first quarter of the year 1873, there were 10, whereas [there] were 21 and 18 in the preceding and succeeding quarters....There was...a similar experience at the County prison, the production of crime as well as of insanity having diminished in a striking manner....The exceptional periods corresponded exactly with the last two 'strikes' in the coal and iron industries" in the county where the asylum and prison were located. It is suggested that "the decrease was undoubtedly due mainly to the fact that the labourers had no money to spend in drinking and in debauchery, that they were sober and temperate by compulsion, the direct result of which was that there was a marked decrease in the production of insanity and of crime."[110] The results indicate that a huge percentage of what looked like mental illness had its origination in alcoholism.

An essential feature of **Borderline Personality Disorder** is "a pervasive pattern of instability of interpersonal relationships, self-image, and affects, and marked impulsivity..." Personal relationships fall apart long before work in the lives of most alcoholics. "Marked impulsivity" is the expected result from damage to the neo-cortex caused by a buildup of acetaldehyde in the brain. Some Personality Types use relationships to inflate their egos, resulting in "frantic efforts to avoid real or imagined abandonment,"[111] which is another indicator of Borderline. In fact, it is symptomatic of alcoholism in some.

**Narcissism** may provide the best example of a listing by the *DSM-IV* of behaviors that appear indistinguishable from those of the practicing alcoholic. A diagnosis of this Disorder requires five or more of the following attributes:

- A grandiose sense of self-importance.
- A preoccupation with "fantasies of unlimited success, power, brilliance, beauty or ideal love."
- A belief that he is "special" and can only be understood by, or associate with, other such persons.

- A need for "excessive admiration."
- "...a sense of entitlement, i.e., unreasonable expectations of especially favorable treatment or automatic compliance with his or her expectations."
- "Is inter-personally exploitative, i.e., takes advantage of others to achieve his or her own ends."
- A lack of empathy.
- Envious of others, or thinks that they are envious of him.
- Displays arrogant and haughty attitudes toward others.[112]

All of these criteria are symptoms of alcoholism. Let's take them one at a time, referring to each in order:

1. This is, essentially, the definition of inflated ego used to describe the self-view of practicing alcoholics ("an inordinately large sense of self-importance").

2. Alcoholics often inform others of yet their latest and greatest scheme or conquest. (Four of the preoccupations listed happen to roughly equate to those that might be expected of each of the four basic human Temperaments. Therefore, a person of any Personality Type as measured by the Myers-Briggs Type Indicator can appear to have Narcissism.)[113]

3. A belief that one is this special requires a high-minded view of self-importance, or inflated ego.

4. Expectations of such admiration also relate to the alcoholic's excessively high opinion of self.

5. A sense of entitlement exemplifies the behavior of the god-like controlling alcoholic, particularly among those seeking political favoritism or power.

6. Addicts, always under the impression that they are more important than is anyone else, exploit others in order to inflate their egos.

7. When addicted, even those who are normally empathic will appear unconcerned with the needs of others; after all, addicts are the center of your universe.

8. Envy, or unreasonable resentments, may be related to euphoric recall, which results in blaming everyone else for one's troubles. After all, the addict, who does no wrong, cannot be to blame for problems in his life or anyone else's. In

addition, having a feeling that he is on par with God may result in a belief that others are envious of him.

9.  The practicing egomaniac addict regularly displays such an arrogant and haughty attitude.

Five out of nine criteria must be met for a diagnosis of Narcissism. However, meeting even one of these should raise suspicions of alcoholism.

Many therapists believe that alcoholism results from Personality Disorders.  However, tests from which we could infer that one might have alcoholism *because* of personality problems have generally been administered during the first few days of abstinence. Recall that when such tests were repeated after three months, 50 to 80% of what appeared to have been Personality Disorders had disappeared.[114] Considering the fact that it takes two or three years for the brain to do most of its healing and for a sense of normalcy to begin to return, we might predict an even greater rate of what some think of as "spontaneous remission" from Personality Disorders as time goes on. Therefore, when "crazy" behaviors are exhibited, we should give the benefit of the doubt and stick with the odds: the person is usually *not* nuts. He's usually alcoholic.

# Myth #65
## "He's no alcoholic; he's just a racist."

Some would consider the late Black Panther Eldridge Cleaver to have been a left-wing racist. Only when he got sober did he have a dramatic change of heart. In his last interview, on "60 Minutes" in early 1998, he was contrite when he admitted, "If people had listened to Huey Newton and me in the 1960s, there would have been a holocaust in this country."[115] He died a registered Republican.

The story of Sven Hermany may be typical of German-type Neo-Nazi skinheads. Hermany began drinking at age 14 and was in trouble from the outset. He destroyed a street lamp and followed that up with crimes progressively more violent, often ending with him shouting "Heil Hitler" at police officers. He was enrolled in a vocational boarding school for troubled students and found it difficult to get out of bed after drinking, "a lot," as he put it, despite rules at the school prohibiting alcohol. At age 21 after drinking all night, he and a friend attacked a black man, William Poku, at a bus stop. Poku believes he escaped only because the two attackers were, as the German police put it, "extremely intoxicated." At his trial Hermany announced, "I am a racist." Appealing to the court later for a lighter sentence, he told the judge he had changed. He was no longer a Nazi and, in a statement suggesting he had put two and two together, he promised to "give up drinking."[116]

There were plenty of clues that the behaviors of Benjamin Smith, who went on a shooting rampage against Jews, Blacks and Asians over 4th of July weekend 1999, might become deadly. In October 1997 he was accused of beating his girlfriend and fighting with other students. Because he had been apprehended for possession of illegal drugs and had spent a year in drug counseling in 1996, he was required to undergo psychological counseling, take an ethics class and perform community service. However he was not required, as a condition of parole, to become abstinent or even to attend AA or Narcotics Anonymous meetings. While reported in newspaper reports after the rampage to have possessed drugs, he was never identified as having alcoholism. His behaviors indicated a particularly virulent form of addiction.

One of the lead articles on the tragedy was titled, "Killer learned hatred during college years." However, few if any other students attending the same college "learned" hatred, especially to this degree. Either they weren't alcohol or other drug addicts, or they didn't have such a toxic form of addiction. Smith's alcoholism caused him to inflate his ego by disparaging other classes of people.[117] We can be thankful that few alcoholics, even those holding entire groups in contempt, go so far as to commit murder.

Many alcoholics are superb at leading. Having a damaged neo-cortex seems to increase the power and ability of the unconscious emotional mind, the limbic system, to tap into the needs and instinctual drives of others. One such urge appears to be a desire to "belong," which is near the top of Abraham Maslow's hierarchy of needs (secondary only to the survival-insuring physiological and safety needs).[118] Since the limbic system is responsible for herding behaviors, it may be hypothesized that those with an inherently weak neo-cortex become more easily inclined to unthinkingly run with the herd. This idea could account for the success of many despots in history, including Adolf Hitler and Jim Jones of Jonestown, Guyana, who lured 900 men, women and children into committing mass suicide via poisoned Kool-Aide. By no means were all or even most of these victims alcoholics. Jones, who was an alcohol and amphetamine addict, could be very convincing.

A friend of Governor George Wallace reported that "'One drink would set him off on a drunk...[and he] wasn't a very pleasant drunk, either...He became belligerent, wanting to fight anything that moved.'"[119] Although he seems to have drunk infrequently, he apparently stopped completely when he realized, "It will cause him to lose control of himself...and something bad will happen."[120] He died "not drinking," with huge support among Blacks, who had before been the targets of his racial epithets.

Some might suggest we shouldn't generalize based on a few incidents. However, statistics are hard to come by when no practicing alcoholic believes he is one. I have known a number of racists and others who used racial slurs, eventually finding alcoholism in almost every case. Readers able to dig deep enough in a suspect's life are unlikely to find many exceptions. Joseph Kennedy, father of President John Kennedy, may have been typical. He sprinkled his speech with black jokes, referred to Indians as "savages," and asked "'Can't you get any white help?'" as he cursed "the hell out of anyone who served him from the wrong side or put one ice cube too many in his Jack Daniels."[121]

# Myth #66
# "He's probably just a harmless 'big talker'."

Being a "big talker" is indicative of having a need to inflate one's ego, which in turn is indicative of alcoholism. If he's alcoholic and not in the latter stages of the disease, he is far from harmless. He's potentially lethal.

The United States initially dismissed Venezuela's megalomaniac de facto dictator, Hugo Chavez, as a "harmless big talker."[122] We dismiss such talk, in which the rich or some other class is blamed for society's problems, at great risk. If policy makers in Washington had understood alcoholism, they might not have underestimated Chavez. His behaviors have threatened stability in the region and subjected millions of Venezuelans to loss of freedom and declining living standards. While there is no definite confirmation yet of alcoholism, he is known to drink ten espresso coffees per day. Unpublished studies seem to suggest a very high correlation between alcoholism and an ability to sleep despite drinking large quantities of caffeine at or near bedtime. There's also a possibility that, like Adolf Hitler, he uses stimulants to get up and barbiturates, alcohol in pill form for the alcoholic, to come down. As alcoholism expert Stanley Gitlow, M.D., said, "It doesn't matter which sedative or tranquilizers an alcoholic uses, including alcohol [or barbiturates]....The exact timing and sequence may be a little different, but [if] you take one and replace it with another—the brain won't know the difference."[123]

Anecdotes, short accounts of real events, usually personal or biographical, are sometimes the best we can do in studying a disease that few are identified as having in the early- to middle-stages. I observed one such "big talker" in a small-town restaurant early one Friday evening, carrying on almost incessantly on his cell phone and flirting with the waitresses between calls. Noting several other behavioral clues to the idea that he may have been under the influence and leaving at about the same time, I wrote down his license plate number. Heading off in the same direction on a rural highway, I was sure I'd see something to report. After driving twenty miles without incident, I figured I must have been wrong about him. However, when he stopped in front of a bar in the next town, my wife commented, "My alcoholic ex-boyfriend did that." Explaining "that" involved bar hopping when driving long distances, I called the Highway Patrol and suggested they watch for him. He was arrested later that evening for DUI after running a red light and apprehended two months later for another DUI. Obviously, he is anything but a "harmless big talker."

## Myth #67
## "Some just lack impulse control."

Many non-addicts, as well as recovering ones, are impulsive. However, practicing alcoholics are often far more so than when in recovery.

The reason can be found in a damaged neo-cortex, which allows the basal ganglia free reign. The violent and sexual impulses of alcoholics who exhibit such loss of control make sense when we realize that the purpose of this "reptilian" brain is survival and procreation. We know to avoid cornering a wild animal. The same can be said for many alcoholics.

The behaviors also take less extreme form in every-day impulses that serve to inflate the ego—the sudden turn from charmer to intimidator and back again, or an instantaneous decision to do something that may not be for the betterment of one's family, employment or mankind. The alcoholic doesn't "just" lack impulse control; alcoholism increases the prevalence of such behavior by allowing the impulses and emotional responses of the lower brain centers to run free of the rational restraints of the neo-cortex.

# Myth #68
## "The behaviors will improve with anger management counseling."

Studies indicate there is no evidence that men who complete domestic-violence counseling programs treat women any better than men who have never taken such a course.[124] One anonymous center that had counseled abusers for several years said they had no successful outcomes. No wonder: they have been attempting to treat symptoms of a disorder, rather than the disorder itself.

The most confusing aspect of domestic violence is the fact that as one counseling center told a victim, "Abusers generally abuse only their family, never outsiders." They are often good, only erratically turning bad. Physical abusers always start out heaping verbal abuse on their victims. After the attack, they apologize and beg to be forgiven. This cycle of behavior is indicative of alcoholism. Therefore, when anger turns into abuse, the underlying disease of alcoholism must be dealt with, successful treatment of which generally results in abuse and anger dissipating. Given the fact that physical abuse is invariably preceded by verbal attacks and most alcoholics are not prone to violence, severe anger by itself also suggests alcoholism, or at least close codependency. In either case, the underlying disorder, not the symptom, needs to be treated.

# Myth #69 (a "half-truth")
## "Power and control are classic signs of a batterer."

Indeed they are—but they are also classic signs of pathological liars, con men and those who verbally abuse others. These are, as we have shown, almost always alcoholics. Therefore, a more apt, useful and accurate statement is "power and control are classic indications of alcoholism," which, as previously described, explains the battery.

# Myth #70 (a "half-truth")
# "He's abusive and probably an alcoholic."

This statement suggests that they're independent of one another. The idea that physical abuse rarely exists without alcoholism is supported by the fact that 85% of perpetrators of domestic violence have a history of alcohol-related problems.[125] And alcoholism is never absent emotional/verbal, physical and/or financial abuse.

This statement can also imply that abuse causes alcoholism. Yet, recovering alcoholics are rarely, if ever, abusive. While abstinent alcoholics can engage in poor behaviors, this usually indicates that they are not in a program of sobriety, working to deflate the ego. The truth of the matter is the reverse: if he's alcoholic, he's abusive.

# Myth #71 (a "half-truth")
# "She has low self-esteem; that doesn't make her an alcoholic."

And she may not be. However, alcoholism causes a loss of self-esteem, or favorable view of self. The longer active addiction continues the greater the likelihood that the addict will eventually remember or experience the effects of behaviors over which she is embarrassed or sickened.

On the other hand, as outside observers, we may be unaware of a lack of self-esteem in another person. What looks like over-confidence is often an inflated ego. This inordinately large sense of self-importance often masks a loss of self-respect. Where a cock-sure, pompous or arrogant attitude is observed, a negative self-view resulting from alcoholic behaviors is often found, but only if we can look deep enough.

## Myth #72
## "He got into trouble because of his drinking."

Drinking does not intrinsically cause problems. However, drinking by alcoholics results in misbehaviors. Poor behaviors cause trouble.

It's essential to use the right words and inject the entire sequence into the equation. Alcoholics think they can drink with the rest of us. They don't like to be told they can't. We might make more headway and get more alcoholics sober if, instead, we explain with video- or audio-taped proof that his drinking causes poor behaviors leading to disasters, rather than leaving room for interpretation. Besides, most don't cause or stumble into trouble due to drinking, because their drinking doesn't cause misbehaviors. We need to distinguish between the two. When in recovery, alcoholics are often told they can't drink. However, *they need to be told that if they drink again, they will at some point act destructively.* This is a very different statement and conveys far more information to a temporarily abstinent or sober alcoholic. When this becomes the phrase of choice, we may see far greater numbers of alcoholics achieving long-term recovery, and at a younger age.

## Myth #73
## "Most people who engage in destructive behaviors are just bad people."

Most are alcoholics first. Recall that a buildup of acetaldehyde causes brain damage. This allows the base survival instincts and impulses of the reptilian brain to reign supreme over the rational thought processes of the neo-cortex. This simple biochemistry causes those with alcoholism to act badly.

David Westerfield, who was convicted in the murder of Danielle van Dam in 2002, is one of those who occasionally exhibited behaviors indicative of an unconstrained limbic system. As television writer Joseph Honig points out, "Those who would damage and murder our children look anything but dangerous or homicidal. Mostly, they are unremarkable in appearance. Some even seem kind and caring." Honig began to make the connection, as he wrote in an open letter to Westerfield, "Yes, you were a drinker capable of private rages." What he didn't explicitly identify was alcoholism, because either he didn't have evidence that Westerfield had lost control over his drinking or wasn't aware that such loss of control occurs only in late-stage alcoholism. He also told Westerfield that "no one in your world understood that [your] anger could prove uncontrollable."[126] But we have no idea which alcoholic's rages will get out of control, or when.

Westerfield was a PTA dad who took his children to baseball games and on camping trips. However, an ex-girlfriend testified that his normally easygoing personality changed when he drank alcohol and that this was, in fact, "one of the reasons they broke up" the year before the trial. He had a conviction for DUI in 1996. Westerfield himself admitted to police that "he was very drunk when he ran into Danielle's mother, Brenda van Dam, at a bar the night of the girl's disappearance."[127] The real David Westerfield, contrary to Honig's feelings, may well have been a decent human being, turned into a monster by the particular way in which his body processed the drug.

If we want apparently bad people to become good, productive members of society, we need to deal with the root of the problem by connecting the dots between bad behaviors and use of the drug. The earlier we do this, the better. As is typical, there were probably dozens or even hundreds of incidents in the life of David Westerfield for which close persons and/or the law could have intervened. A child's life might have been saved.

We need to do all we can to coerce abstinence in those suspected of having alcoholism. This might include regular testing for alcohol and other drugs in order to be offered early parole, or to keep a job or a driver's license. This doesn't mean that the judge should say, "You can't drink and drive." It means instead that he explains with a sincere and caring tone, "When you drink, you suffer a series of chemical reactions that damages the rational, human part of the brain. This leads to pre-civilized behaviors and makes you act like you think you are God. In turn, you develop a sense of invincibility, which makes you do things like get behind the wheel of a car while under the influence. I'll give odds that this God-complex makes you act badly in other areas of your life as well. And, since I never want to see you again, you can no longer use alcohol or any other mood-altering drug." In other words, the "war on drugs" needs to be narrowed in scope, concentrating only on those who act badly as a result of use.

## Myth #74
## "I'm a recovering alcoholic and I'm still bad."

In the course of a special presentation to a chemical dependency class, I pointed out that addiction causes poor behaviors, which usually dissipate in sobriety. One student responded that he'd been in recovery for several years and was still "bad." I retorted that even if true, he wasn't nearly as big a wrongdoer as when he was using. Insisting otherwise, he left the door open to the idea that bad behaviors cause alcoholism, which suggests that if he learned to control his conduct he could drink safely. I looked at him square in the face and said, "You don't even remember most of what you did when you were a practicing alcoholic, because you were in a blackout half of the time. When you weren't in a blackout, you suffered from euphoric recall, putting a self-favoring light on everything you did. I'll repeat my assertion: you aren't nearly as 'bad' now as when you were drinking." Over the course of the next ten or twenty seconds, during which the entire class was silent, his resistance to the idea melted. Humbled, he admitted that I was right.

This is not to suggest there aren't a few innately bad people. However, recovering alcoholics are far less likely to act on their impulses in destructive ways than when using. As one member of AA was quoted in the Big Book of Alcoholics Anonymous, "If everyone [could be in AA], there would be no need for jails."[128] He is not far from correct. The rate of recidivism is very low among those who make a decision—and keep their promise—never to drink or use again. This is true even for those initially coerced into a program of abstinence. Alabama offers a choice to all prisoners who test positive for drugs when they are booked: "Forced drug rehab in a prison drug facility or a longer sentence with the general population." Those in the program must undergo regular drug testing when released and failure results in being sent back to prison. Twice as many criminals participating in the forced program remain drug-free than those who have not gone through the program.[129]

## Myth #75
## "People can change—they just hardly ever do."

This is one of the most pernicious myths when applied to alcoholics.

Most think that criminals are innately evil. It's difficult to imagine that a Jeffrey Dahmer might have been a decent person, especially for the victims and their families. Yet, if we stop active addiction early enough in its progression, we may be able to prevent the ultimate crimes and tragedies from occurring. If we are to do so early and unequivocally, we need to accept the idea that decent people can become monsters when alcoholism is triggered, and bad seeds can turn far worse. Understanding this at the gut level helps us to offer uncompromising tough love at or near the onset of the disease and, at the same time, maintain optimism based on the reality that people do change—when their brain chemistry changes. Redemption is possible and, in fact, probable for those in recovery.

Most people who act badly are not fundamentally bad. As has been repeatedly maintained, they are usually alcohol and other drug addicts. Addiction causes brain damage, resulting in misbehaviors. If the person becomes sober there is a good chance the brain will heal, allowing the neo-cortex to again exert restraint over the lower brain centers. If this occurs, we will likely observe a dramatic improvement in behaviors. In instances where this does not occur, there was usually a particularly abusive alcoholic parent.

When good behaviors inexplicably change, hardly anyone identifies the root cause. This may have been the case for a "world-class" young entrepreneur working for Wilson Harrell, publisher of *Success* magazine, who wrote, "Self esteem oozed from every fiber of his being…He had it all—including my job, sometime in the future, if everything worked out."

However, he "got involved with a very fast-living group" and began snorting cocaine. We might note that he likely "got involved" because he already experienced the sense of invincibility that only an alcoholic can feel from the use of alcohol. Six months later, Harrell says, he "was no longer the same man." Within a few more months, Harrell "witnessed a horrifying transformation. At first, he missed appointments. Then there were days he didn't show up at all. As with Jekyll and Hyde, even his appearance changed…His moods were erratic and unpredictable…[and he blamed] everyone and everything for his failures, which multiplied."[130]

The fact that so many believe that bad people hardly ever change is perpetuated by the desire of alcoholics to remain anonymous in recovery. This is unfortunate because we are never made aware of the fact that the lovely couple next door may have been out-of-control addicts a dozen years ago. Ask any recovering addict with ten or more years' sobriety whether you would have recognized him while he was a practicing addict. The response will always be a thunderous "no." The behaviors are night and day.

# Myth #76
## "You're either born with a conscience or you're not."

The alternative is "environment or upbringing determines whether a person has a conscience." This is at least partially true, since a child of an addict may be so brutally abused that a sense of morality is beaten from him. However, few others lack such a sense—until alcoholism is triggered. Reprehensible behavior is rare without benefit of innate brain chemistry which, only when combined with alcohol or some other psychotropic drug, allows the lower brain centers freedom from rational restraint.

The start of addictive use of drugs formed a clear demarcation between good behaviors and horrifying ones in the case of Jeremy Strohmeyer. The L.A. Times (July 19, 1998) reported that up to his mid-teen years, Strohmeyer maintained a 3.5 grade point average and planned to attend military college. He built his own computer, wrote poetry and shared a passion for flying with his father. One teacher said that he was in the top one per cent of good kids. *Then* he began drinking.

This is when Jeremy's classmates began to see a violent temper emerge. He spit in a jock's face and mouthed profanities at a hostess after being asked to leave a party. Yet, when drinking heavily with friends who appeared "sloppy" drunk, he seemed relatively sober. His parents couldn't tell when he'd been drinking even though he often reached what had to be at least a moderately high blood alcohol level. This is an excellent sign of alcoholic biochemistry.

He bragged about his sexual exploits and was arrested for drunk driving. With his Internet password "kill," he logged on to countless pornographic sites, downloading hundreds of pictures of children having sex with adults. With his parents losing control, he agreed to see a therapist who, incredibly, prescribed the amphetamine Dexadrine.

Strohmeyer was adopted. His biological parents were reported to be addicts and his adoptive parents were never given the tools to deal with the inherited disease of addiction. A year and a half after his personality began to mutate, Jeremy Strohmeyer committed the unconscionable act of cruelly murdering seven-year-old Sherrice Iverson in a Las Vegas casino. Close persons might have been able to prevent this tragedy had they understood that addiction causes profound personality changes, which can, in a few unpredictable cases, turn monstrous. This capriciousness is the reason that if such changes are observed one should suspect alcoholism and promptly intervene, before it's too late.

## Myth #77
## "She's just accident-prone."

Practicing alcoholics, especially those of certain underlying personality types, tend to take greater risks than do non-alcoholics. Engaging in reckless behavior is one of the ways by which the alcoholic inflates her ego. Even though many early-stage alcoholics function well when under the influence, the number of risks they take significantly increases the odds of accidents.

Various workplace studies have concluded that 50 to 90% of on-the-job accidents are precipitated by alcohol. Such events declined by 82% after treating employees identified as having alcoholism at the Lansing, Michigan Oldsmobile plant.[131] Addicts were found to be 3.6 times more likely to injure themselves or another person in the workplace and were also deemed responsible for about 40% of all industrial fatalities.[132]

The percentage of drowning deaths attributable to alcohol is estimated at 70%, while 90% of fatalities from fire involve alcohol.[133] B.D. Hyman reported that her alcoholic mother, actress Bette Davis, set her own bed on fire several times with cigarettes, which she chain-smoked.[134] A study of snowmobile accidents in Wisconsin reported that as many as 70% were related to the equivalent of DUIs among snowmobile drivers. Other studies have found that addicts are five times more likely than are non-addicts to file workers' compensation claims.[135]

Statistics such as these are especially compelling given the fact that many early-stage alcoholics are not even identified as such. They also lend support to the idea that absent other variables, 80% of automobile accidents may be addiction-related (on-road factors such as inclement weather and road hazards are probably considerably more dangerous than workplace ones). Noelle Bush, governor Jeb Bush's daughter, had been involved in five traffic accidents since 1993 prior to her arrest for prescription fraud at age 24.[136] The second accident in a relatively short period of time should clue us in to a fairly high probability of alcohol and/or other drug addiction.

The degree to which alcoholism increases the likelihood of having an accident is significantly greater than it would appear to the casual observer. The fact that half of all road fatalities are alcohol or other-drug related doesn't begin to give a sense of the increased odds. Consider the fact that not only are the vast majority of DUIs alcoholics, but also that alcoholics consist of only 10% or so of the population. The average addict gets behind the wheel of a car while under the influence about 80 times per year, comprising at most one-fifth the number of times she drives and, therefore, a fifth of all her miles. Since a fifth of 10% is two per cent, nearly 50% of fatalities are likely the result of the two per cent of all road miles driven by the legally intoxicated, almost all of whom are alcoholics.

Now, reverse the idea. If there's a fatality or, arguably, any injury accident, the odds that one of the participants is under the influence and, therefore, an alcoholic, is about 50%, which doesn't include alcoholics between drinking episodes. The accident-prone *may* be just that. However, since the probabilities are at least 50-50 that someone involved in a serious incident has alcoholism, the odds are probably far greater for those repeatedly involved in "accidents."

## Myth #78
## "He's just a bad driver, not DUI."

A National Highway Traffic Safety Administration (NHTSA) study linked driving behaviors to probabilities of driving under the influence.[137] The odds of DUI in someone committing many on-the-road misbehaviors are surprisingly high. For example, the odds are 50% for someone tailgating or stopping without cause in a traffic lane and 45% for those unnecessarily or erratically braking or backing into traffic. We might not think twice about seeing someone make an illegal U-turn; after all, most sober drivers have probably committed this infraction a number of times. However, the key to understanding the surprisingly high odds of driving misbehaviors in alcoholics is that they engage in such conduct far more frequently than do non-alcoholics. This is the reason the probability of DUI was 35% for any one illegal U-turn.[138]

Recovering alcoholics, when they remember what they did while in their disease, recount the numerous misbehaviors committed both on the road and off. Some admit to behaviors every bit as loathsome between drinking episodes. Many practicing alcoholics have a "the rules don't apply to me" attitude, whether drinking or not. This is the reason he's probably not "just" a bad driver, but instead a likely DUI or an alcoholic between drinking episodes.

# Myth #79
## "She's not DUI.
## She's probably just having a bad day."

We often figure that a driver is just having a bad day when he cuts or flips someone off, or yells a profanity. Yet, cutting someone off is one form of failing to yield the right-of-way, for which the NHTSA study showed a 45% probability of DUI. Moreover, DUIs made 60% of obscene gestures. Therefore, about half of those commonly ascribed as "having a bad day" are not; they are alcoholics, having what is for them, a normal day. And, this doesn't include alcoholics between drinking episodes, whose behavior can be as awful as when drinking. It is not unreasonable to suggest the possibility that there is very little bad conduct, on the road or off, that cannot be ascribed to active alcoholics, whether or not high at the time.

Road rage is an even more extreme behavior. While we have no hard statistics on road rage and likelihood of DUI, we do have such statistics on its in-the-sky equivalent, disruptive airline passengers. A probability of DUI well over

50% by those engaging in road rage can be extrapolated from an airline industry study.[139] Disruptive airline passengers leading to pilot errors had consumed an "excess" of alcohol in 43% of such instances. An additional 8% were on "other drugs or prescription medications," which we can assume to be psychotropic drugs capable of causing distortions of perception and memory in susceptible individuals. Since the "excess" of alcohol consumed involved only those who were observed drinking heavily, there may have been an additional substantial contingent whose heavy use went unnoticed. This is suggested by the fact that an additional nine per cent of such incidents were linked to passengers smoking in lavatories. Since 90% of alcoholics smoke and these smokers were engaging in their habit when forbidden and potentially dangerous, they exhibited classic signs of alcoholism and were possibly under the influence. Another 15% involved fighting over use of prohibited electronic devices and five per cent were bomb or hijack threats. Since there is a high (80 to 90%) probability that potentially violent incidents involve an addict (intoxicated or not), we're up to almost 80% of such events involving likely addicts.

Road rage is no different in principle than its in-the-sky equivalent. While 100% of the latter are investigated, relatively few of those exhibiting rage while driving are even contacted by authorities, much less tested. A number of Drug Recognition Experts, the elite law enforcers trained to detect drugs in the system by observing physical indicators, believe that alcohol plays a significant and probably vastly under-recognized role in road rage, as well as in those drivers having a "bad day."

## Myth #80
## "He may be an alcoholic, but he would never risk a child's life by drinking and driving with one."

According to a recent study, "two-thirds of alcohol-related motor-vehicle deaths among child passengers are a result of drinking by the child's own driver."[140] Another study found that "more than half of elementary school-aged children [killed] in alcohol-related crashes were not with a drunken teenager," but instead were being driven by a person "of parent age who was intoxicated."[141]

When tempted to think that no person would do such a thing, consider the fact that addicts are responsible for 85% of domestic violence. Such abuse is committed against people who, by definition, are personally and often intimately known. Many addicts, some of whom engage in violence against those whom in their right minds they would never harm, are not likely to think twice about driving under the influence with children in the vehicle.

## Myth #81
## "She would never hurt anyone."

After the murder-suicide of comedian Phil Hartman by his wife Brynn, friends were shocked that she would even hurt someone, much less kill. Yet, we should think "unpredictable" and assume that we cannot know how destructive an active addict's behavior may become, or when, regardless of how well we know the person. Addiction changes behaviors. Every addict violates values he or she may hold dear when sober. A practicing addict is capable of anything, tragically proven time and again.

## Myth #82
## "He'd *never* do *that!*"

Who would have dreamt that Rush Limbaugh, the anti-drug and pro war-on-drugs crusading talk-show host, would himself be taking illegally obtained drugs in quantities that could kill a non-addict? Who would think that the musically brilliant and seemingly gentle Michael Jackson could engage in questionable (and possibly criminal) acts with young children? Yet, if he is addicted—for which there are numerous behavioral indications—he is capable of anything, including monstrously heinous acts. As we have seen, brilliance, success and even an otherwise gentle personality are no impediment to alcohol and other drug addiction and, therefore, to the commission of horrifying sins.

## Myth #83
## "Law enforcers can always be trusted to tell the truth and act appropriately."

The predisposed person usually develops alcoholism in the early teen years, average age thirteen. He generally selects an occupation in his later teens or beyond. At some conscious or subconscious level he asks, "What profession will allow me to inflate my ego?" Those with alcoholism from lower- to middle-income America often find they can inflate theirs by wielding power over thugs as police officers or prison guards. Those from middle- to upper-income levels may see the potential for ego inflation as prosecutors, judges and politicians. This may explain why so many law enforcers have alcoholism. Alcoholics are far more likely than are non-alcoholics to wield power capriciously over citizens, defendants, convicts and constituents. The "code of silence" so prevalent in law enforcement allows the behaviors—impelled by alcoholism—to continue unchecked.

Characterized by erratically bad behaviors, we have seen that alcoholism often takes form in dishonesty, copious lying, adultery and betrayal. Many alcoholics can be trusted some of the time, but few, if any, all of the time. And while we may be able to trust in one sphere of life, we don't know which area, which alcoholic, or when, regardless of how prestigious the profession.

Author James Graham relates a classic account of dishonesty, lying and deceit in the story of Charles Whitman, District

Attorney of New York, who framed police lieutenant Charles Becker for murder.[142] Using false witnesses and suborning perjury, Whitman was able to convict Becker, but only at a second trial. The first conviction was overturned by the Court of Appeals, which stated that the case rested on the testimony of six witnesses, three of whom were "indisputably...guilty of the murder...."[143] The Governor of New York at the time of the trial was convinced of Becker's innocence and intended to commute the death sentence.[144] Unfortunately for both Becker and American justice, Whitman was elected Governor of New York when the lieutenant landed on Death Row. On the day before the execution, Whitman falsely accused Becker of murdering his first wife.[145] When his current wife asked Whitman for a stay on the eve of the execution, the Governor was so inebriated that, as she later told a reporter, two assistants physically supported him the entire time and he was "in no condition to understand anything I said."[146] Becker was executed. Whitman's alcoholism soon became apparent even to the public, a result of which was a failed re-election bid.[147]

We should not fall under the misconception that this sort of story, or less repugnant versions, does not occur every day in America. Alcoholics are often too conniving to get caught, even in a system with extraordinary checks and balances. Until we become more aware of the behaviors that alcoholics are capable of and eliminate the voice in our heads that tells us, "Oh, but *my* alcoholic would *never* do such a thing," such tragic sagas will be repeated time and again. Likewise, we need to expunge the idea that because a person is a law enforcer, he couldn't possibly be an alcoholic and, therefore, capable of criminal activity. Drug Recognition Experts estimate that 20% of big-city cops and up to 50% of those on smaller police forces have alcoholism, who are, therefore, capable of anything.

Trouble among law enforcers can almost always be attributed to the behaviors caused by this disease. Former LAPD officer Ruben Palomares, suspected of running a ring of robbers, may be one of these. Palomares and his cohorts used squad cars during rampages in which they allegedly beat up blacks and committed a string of robberies. Drug Enforcement

Agency personnel are said to have found a money-counting machine at Palomares' home, along with semi-automatic assault rifles, after which he pleaded guilty to cocaine trafficking. The conjecture was that the criminal behavior began because, while off-duty with a shoulder injury, he "began abusing alcohol and pain pills."[148] Readers will note that this likely occurred long after addiction had been triggered.

Recovering addict ex-cons with no apparent grudge to bear, along with a number of retired prison guards and chemical dependency experts familiar with the prison system suggest that the number of addicted correctional officers is 50 to 80%, depending on the prison. There is, of course, no way to confirm this or any other similar statistic, since no one admits to being an alcoholic until he is sober. Only then do we hear, "Thank God I'm an alcoholic, because when I was using, I wasn't." There is little doubt that 80 to 90% of incarcerated prisoners have alcoholism.[149] A system in which pre-mammalian, reptilian impulses in police officers, prison guards and prisoners alike are unconstrained by the neo-cortex is not one designed to reduce the rate of recidivism. If we hope to decrease the odds of encountering problems, we need to intervene in the lives of practicing addicts as early in the progression of the disease as possible. Doing this among law enforcers throughout the entire judicial and political systems could do more to improve the human condition than any other action.

## Myth #84
## "Poverty causes crime."

If poverty caused crime, there would never have been an Enron and L. Dennis Kozlowski would not have allegedly engaged in flagrantly abusive and excessive behaviors while chairman of Tyco. (How else to describe charging a $6,000 shower curtain, a $38,000 backgammon table and a $103,000 antique mirror at shareholders' expense?)[150] Nor would con artists such as Charles Ponzi continue to bilk investors after creating great wealth at the expense of their victims.

The term "white collar crime" was coined by criminologist Edwin Sutherland in 1939, after observing that many successful professionals committed criminal acts. Since poverty could not be the primary risk factor, Sutherland concluded that such crime must be learned behavior, a consequence of corporate culture. Yet, by far the vast majority of those in this culture do not "learn" to behave badly. And, we have seen that 80 to 90% of criminal behavior is fueled by the alcohol-soaked basal ganglia compelling the addict to have a need to inflate the ego by wielding power capriciously. Wealth does not change biochemistry and alcoholism is an equal-opportunity disease. Therefore, we could easily surmise that crime, regardless of style, consists of reptilian impulses riding roughshod over the neo-cortex.

Just as wealth, position and other factors determine the form that alcoholism takes, they also help decide the style of criminal behaviors in which the afflicted engages. The alcoholic growing up in the ghetto often physically overpowers his victims, while the addict graduating from Harvard may wield power over constituents or shareholders in less obvious ways.

## Myth #85
## "In the end, we can negotiate with a madman."

When we attempt to negotiate with someone who appears to be crazy, we are usually dealing with an alcohol or other drug addict. Although ignored or considered irrelevant by most historians and biographers, addiction can be found in almost every tyrannical dictator in history. Peter the Great, Ivan the Terrible, Henry the Vlll and Joseph Stalin were alcoholics. Adolf Hitler was addicted to both amphetamines and barbiturates. Saddam Hussein and Kim Jong Il of North Korea are likely alcoholics.

Ask a recovering addict, not with just a few but rather fifteen years of sobriety what he might have been capable of had he been in a position of power while drinking or using, and the response will often be "anything."

Attempting to negotiate with a brain affected by alcoholism is like trying to be rational with a reptile. Only brute force stopped Hitler; only death stopped Stalin, who many believe was setting the stage for a third World War. Non-interventionists may wish to rethink their position when considering how best to deal with totalitarian dictators having access to weapons of mass destruction. We cannot negotiate with chemistry.

The same is true in our private affairs. The brain of the practicing alcoholic, soaked in acetaldehyde, is not a rational one. The addict cannot see that his troubles extend any further than your toes, which he will crush if given the opportunity. When dealing with madness, we must simply lay down rules, step aside and follow through with promises made.

# 6

# Consequences

## Myth #86
## "If alcoholism is a disease, the afflicted should not be held responsible for behaviors."

There are many paradoxes about alcoholism. The most fundamental is the highly functional overachieving alcoholic. The second is the relationship between alcoholism as a disease and accountability for one's actions.

In a sense, alcoholism is like diabetes, in which the afflicted must limit the intake of sugar in order to manage the disease. However, since a person with alcoholism, in the long run, cannot control the behaviors resulting from use, he can never drink safely. And, because the drug makes him act badly while it makes him feel, as author William Faulkner put it, superlative, he typically needs to be coerced into abstinence.

One could argue that prohibition is the answer. However, the problem is not the drug. Most people can use alcohol (along with other drugs) and not misbehave. Therefore rather than the drug, we need to target the *person* on the drug. Since "targeted prohibition" must be linked to misbehaviors, the person with alcoholism needs to experience proper consequences. In order to inspire a desire in the predisposed to want to stop, he *must* be held accountable for poor behaviors.

Those who vociferously maintain that alcoholism is not a

disease may do so out of a desire to insure that the law isn't twisted to excuse alcoholics for misbehaviors. The idea that alcoholism, even though genetic, must *never* be used to excuse poor conduct needs to be codified. Regardless of whether it is a disease, the treatment is the same: uncompromising disenabling not only by those close, but also by society, in ways that require the addict to bear complete responsibility for his actions.

# Myth #87
# "Friends don't let friends plead guilty."

The idea that we should make someone suffer seems contrary to humanistic principles. Yet, the highest form of humanity that we can offer the guilty is to lovingly subject them to the consequences of their misbehaviors.

However, while non-addicts are capable of quickly learning from errors in judgment when forced to live with the outcome, alcoholics are far less able to do so. The human part of the brain, which learns from experience, becomes subordinate to the undamaged lower brain centers, which cannot. How, then, can the imposition of responsibility help the practicing addict?

While he is unable to connect the dots on his own, infliction of consequences helps cause a buildup of crises. This sets the stage for intervention, in which those close offer a choice of sobriety or further consequences. Therefore, pain from logical outcomes is the addict's best friend. The most effective consequence may be an arrest for DUI or other crime in which he is encouraged to plead guilty.[151] Another is by turning state's evidence when needed to convict. While watching this may hurt the rest of us, the continuing misbehaviors of the practicing alcoholic promise to wreak far greater pain on those with whom he comes into contact in the long run. Ultimately, this includes himself.

If imprisoned, the odds do not favor sobriety. The criminal justice system, in which punishment rather than rehabilitation is the declared goal, is not designed to reduce the rate of recidivism among alcoholics. While non-alcoholics may engage in—and be arrested for—misbehavior once, some alcohol and other drug addicts commit repeated criminal acts for as long as they use. Therefore, the goal must be appropriate consequences *with* rehabilitation, doing everything we can to discourage use. The most effective way of doing this might be to offer early release and parole in exchange for regular and random testing.

## Myth #88
## "If she's an alcoholic, she would have lost her job."

People with whom the alcoholic comes into contact are often injured, killed or lured into the maelstrom of insanity characteristic of addiction long before the alcoholic meets her bottom. Successful ego inflation and damage to others go hand in hand.

There are three ways by which to inflate the ego, paradoxical in terms of outcomes. The first is to wield power over others, especially capriciously. This is harmful to other people, whether inflicted by domestic terrorists in one's home, on-road terrorists, or international ones. In the workplace, those falsely accused of improprieties or incompetence may lose their jobs long before the addict loses hers.

The second is to act recklessly. This can result in tragedy, as when Henri Paul drove 90 miles per hour in a 30-MPH zone to escape the paparazzi. Or, it can lead to new discoveries, as has likely been the case when only extraordinary risk-taking could solve a problem or resolve an issue. This may have been the case for small groups of men on tiny boats in vast oceans discovering new lands. It is doubtful, also, whether news station CNN and its progeny would exist today, were it not for the uncommon risk-taking of one who shows a number of indications of alcoholism, Ted Turner.

The third way is to achieve. This can in some cases lead to enormous success both for the alcoholic and others, even though doing good things for mankind is not the goal of the practicing alcoholic (regardless of his claims). In millions of lesser cases, inflating the ego keeps alcoholics working at their jobs. As author James Graham points out, successful ego inflation may help stave off the otherwise inevitable progression into latter-stage alcoholism for decades. This is why work is typically the last domino to fall as the alcoholic wreaks havoc all around.

This explains the fact that an estimated 85% of alcoholics hold jobs. Alcoholism often becomes obvious only in retirement. For example, the contrast in alcoholic behaviors among law enforcers pre- and post-retirement is rumored pronounced.

This could also account for the observation that women in the recent past tended to move more rapidly into middle- and late-stage alcoholism than did men.[152] They were less likely to hold jobs and, hence, less able to inflate the ego through their work.

# Myth #89 (a "half-truth")
# "He can't keep drinking—
# it'll kill him, and that would be tragic."

Indeed it would—but the inference is that tragedy hasn't already occurred.

By the time comments like this are made about someone's drinking, there have usually been hundreds of incidents and numerous lesser tragedies for which close persons or the law could have intervened, but didn't. The alcoholic has probably ruined personal and professional relationships, suffered emotional disorders, engaged in reckless conduct risking others' lives and committed misbehaviors that have infringed upon the rights of others. His body, miracle of engineering that it is, usually suffers last.

On the other hand it's never too late to coerce the abstinence from which sobriety grows. Many recovering alcoholics have said in their dying moments, "Thank God I got sober. I got to know my family, even if it was only for a year or two. And, they now know that the drug-crazed monster they thought was me, wasn't."

## Myth #90
## "We have to wait for her to hit rock-bottom."

Alcoholics must "hit bottom" before having a desire to get sober. However, onlookers need not wait. They can help create the motivation by initiating and prodding the process.

The look and feel of a "bottom" is in the eye of the alcoholic beholder. Just as every addict has his own style of addiction, each needs his own inducement for sobriety. The character and degree of pain the alcoholic must experience varies from relatively little to extraordinary, sometimes ending in death. By shortening the period of active alcoholism, we reduce the time period during which tragedies are likely to occur, thereby reducing their number. Our goal, then, should be to do everything we can to hasten the trajectory, regardless of the level of pain that we may feel is appropriate, so long as it is not life threatening.

Aside from an understanding of Psychological Type and temperament, which can help us predict the sort of pain that may drive the addict into sobriety, we cannot determine the degree of pain required. Therefore, we need to impose consequences — usually a painful experience for the sober among us to behold — whenever the opportunity arises. This helps to create crises, setting the stage for an intervention in which a chemical dependency expert leads close friends, family and/or work associates in offering life-enhancing promises to the alcoholic.

The threat of spending time in prison often provides requisite pain. Charlie Sheen's father, recovering alcoholic Martin Sheen, understands this. Charlie violated parole by using drugs after a plea of no contest in 1997 for assaulting a girlfriend. A condition of parole was to stay away from drugs. A year later, Charlie almost died from a cocaine overdose. After recovering in the hospital, he went into rehab but walked out the first night. When the elder Sheen heard this, he had the district attorney issue an arrest warrant for violating parole. Charlie was given the choice of confinement in drug rehab or jail. He wisely chose rehab and was required to wear an electronic ankle cuff to make sure he didn't stray (a great way to help deflate that massive alcoholic ego). Charlie says that when he got out of rehab this time, he knew he had to stay sober or return to prison. Acknowledging that Dad had been crafty in using the law, the one thing he could not escape, Charlie explained that coercing abstinence in this way is "why it worked." He also said he knew that his dad loved him.[153]

The longer we wait to intervene in the addict's life, the greater the odds of tragedy occurring. As mentioned, the typical alcoholic drinks beyond the legal limit and gets behind the wheel of a car 80 times per year. Alcoholics create roughly half the carnage on roads and highways, despite the fact that they comprise only 10% of the population and most are not under the influence every time they drive. By some estimates, 40% of divorces involve alcoholism in one spouse or the other. The average alcoholic has a life span 14 years shorter than the typical non-alcoholic, and his alcoholism causes or aggravates some 350 diseases and disorders. These are not the types of bottoms for which we should sit around and wait.

## Myth #91
### "The fact that millions overcome addiction on their own is evidence that alcoholism is not biological and genetic, since they just 'decide' to give it up for no apparent reason."

As with colds and flus, addicts can get better (i.e., decide not to use) by themselves. However, there is almost always external coercion applied — not treatment in the usual sense, but instead a credible threat of consequences for poor behaviors caused by use.

Ask a recovering alcoholic what caused him to get sober

and he will often respond, "I simply had enough," "I was tired of the drinking," or "I decided to find God." However, keep asking. The addict often doesn't know that there is another answer until asked to ponder deeply, sometimes for an extended period.

Time is required for the brain to heal. While most destructive behaviors, along with those that look like Personality Disorders dissipate within the first few months of recovery, true normalcy typically doesn't appear for five to ten years. Even then, the addict may not recollect many of the events during his drinking and using career because of blackouts and euphoric recall. Therefore, we usually have to probe to uncover the truth.

I once asked a highly intelligent alcoholic with 14 years sobriety what caused him to enter into recovery. When he responded with the "I found God" reason, I explained while that is a *way* to get sober, it is not a *reason* to do so. Suggesting he had developed this need because of a tragedy in his life, he couldn't think of anything in particular. I suggested that he consider the possibility.

A year later I asked him the same question. He murmured in a somewhat perplexed tone that he finally remembered. "I was fired and then relegated to a series of demeaning jobs beneath my ability. This was the series of incidents that inspired in me a need to clean up, which I did after a couple of years trying. God gave me the tragedy and then helped get me sober. If I hadn't been fired, I'd probably be dead."

Recall the simple biochemistry. The build-up of the poison that causes brain damage resulting in destructive behaviors also makes the person with alcoholism feel indescribably good. Because of this, he does not decide to stop drinking without reason. We need to provide that motivation—not by trying to reason with him, but rather by simply stating the consequences and imposing them without discussion, argument, debate or negotiation. If this treatment seems reminiscent of the sort Rudolf Dreikurs, M.D. recommends in his book, *Children: the Challenge*, it is.[154] When we encounter addicts, we deal with adolescent mindsets. Recovering alcoholics, usually with at

least five years' sobriety, admit they stopped growing emotionally the day they triggered their alcoholism: average age,
twelve or thirteen.

## Myth #92
## "The fact that she voluntarily went into a facility for rehabilitation is an act of courage."

This direct quote from a source close to six-time Grammy winner Whitney Houston[155] highlights the stunning mythology
surrounding the rehab process. Few addicts voluntarily go into
rehab. If they do, they've already suffered untold tragedy.
More likely, they are dragged in, kicking and screaming.

The truth of the matter is that near the end of a several-hour
intervention during which time Houston adamantly refused
rehabilitation, her family pulled its trump card and threatened
to have authorities remove 11-year-old daughter Bobbi
Kristina. After Whitney blasted them with "four-letter words,
throwing ashtrays and slamming doors," no one budged from
their position. Whitney went into rehab.[156]

## Myth #93
## "When stopped for a traffic violation, most of those driving under the influence are arrested."

The National Highway Traffic Safety Administration study
linking driving behaviors to probabilities of DUI showed that
few of those under the influence are apprehended for DUI,
even when stopped by law enforcers. The U.S. Department of
Transportation somberly stated, "Some officers are not highly
skilled at [DUI] detection. They fail to arrest many [DUI] violators."[157]

Traffic violators cited by police but not suspected of DUI
were ready to get back on the road when researchers administered breath tests. One would think that for every ten DUIs the

original citing officers arrested, researchers might find two or three more. After all, the police are highly trained, close enough to smell the breath and are able to observe behaviors. Those under the influence are thought to lack the ability to multi-task. Therefore, when officers request driver's license, proof of registration and insurance, along with asking, "where are you headed to?" the DUI is normally identified. Or so we would think.

It turns out, the researchers didn't find just two or three more DUIs, or even ten or twenty. For every ten drivers the officers arrested, researchers identified 37 more that should have been. Officers 23% (10 out of 47), researchers (and alcoholics) 77% (37 out of 47).

Most non-alcoholics with even a moderate BAL don't stand a chance at a sobriety checkpoint, or when pulled over for an unrelated violation. Without the alcoholic's high tolerance, they often appear inebriated at BALs below the legal limit. The fact that many recovering alcoholics relate stories of being pulled over on numerous occasions, yet never arrested for DUI, is further evidence that there is obviously something different about the way their bodies process the drug.

## Myth #94
## "We shouldn't concentrate on DUIs when there are so many worse crimes committed."

Why wait for worse crimes to be perpetrated? Driving under the influence is the one infraction in which almost every addict engages with regularity. While felonies are rarely committed, a person who has engaged in criminal activity or ruined relationships, conned friends and/or destroyed families has generally driven while intoxicated hundreds if not thousands of times. It's an overlooked opportunity to intervene and coerce abstinence before worse transgressions, including serious ethical violations, are committed.

The alleged stabbing to death of a 13-year-old boy by

Tamara K. Bohler provides an example in which an arrest and proper consequences for DUI might have saved a life. Bohler was arrested in July 2003 as she reportedly sat on a curb, bleeding and bewildered. She had allegedly attacked her former boyfriend, Jean Marc Weber, and killed his son, Alex. While the motive for the attack "remained under investigation," we are told at the very end of the story that "she had spent a day in jail in April for drunk driving."[158] We who understand alcoholism know that motive is unnecessary when the lower brain centers run amok, unrestrained by the neo-cortex. We also know that if she hadn't been "bewildered" she probably wouldn't have committed the atrocity.

Those driving under the influence are rarely apprehended, much less forced to become abstinent. The average driver engaging in this violation is stopped and arrested only once in every 500 incidents of DUI at best, 2,000 at worst.[159] Because of the success of organizations such as Mothers Against Drunk Driving, very few non-alcoholics drive while under the influence. Since the typical alcoholic is estimated to drive with a BAL in excess of the legal limit 80 times per year, he goes six to twenty-five years between arrests.[160]

Yet, many addicts report they got sober at least in part because of the financial, professional and personal problems occasioned by an arrest for DUI. A conviction can be used to coerce abstinence. The power to offer reduced penalties and a quicker return of one's license and freedom in exchange for blood- and urine-tested sobriety could be used. "How am I driving?" bumper stickers such as those used on many trucks might be required on vehicles owned by a violator. These stickers have reportedly helped reduce fatalities caused by truckers by as much as 50%. The I Saw You Safety & Scholarship Foundation, Inc., has spearheaded an effort by concerned parents to require "My Parents Want to Know How I'm Driving" bumper stickers for vehicles of all 16- and 17-year-old students with high school parking lot privileges. The results of this experiment are nothing short of astounding. After the first year and a half with 500 participants, there were no accidents. Admittedly, this is a self-selected group with obviously non-addicted (or recovering addict) parents who are, therefore, less likely to have addicted children. However, the average rate of accidents for those age 16 is 42% *per year*. This Foundation is adding a program in parts of Michigan and Florida with "The Judge Wants to Know How I'm Driving" stickers as a "Scarlet Letter" condition of probation (which all states allow except New York, Illinois and California).[161] The evidence suggests that the rate of recovery will dramatically improve when this sort of program is made routine.

# Myth #95 (a "half-truth")
## "Drug use is a victimless crime."

Indeed, by itself, it is. However, when used by alcohol and other drug addicts, there are *always* victims.

This does not mean that use itself should be prohibited by force of law. Compelling arguments for treating other drugs in the same way as alcohol have been made by many observers. These include: 1. Increased risk resulting from illegality drives prices far higher than would result in a free market, causing non-participants to be caught in crossfire over turf. 2. These high prices result in extraordinary profits, which allow some of the most despicable people alive to become billionaires. 3. Attempted enforcement of prohibition leads to the creation of innumerable laws, further eroding civil liberties. 4. Extraordinary profits lead to corruption at the highest levels of law enforcement. 5. A person has a right to ingest whatever he wants. After all, it's his body, not society's.

A point not made elsewhere is that the problem is not the drug, but rather the person on the drug. It matters not whether purchased in a liquor store, from a pharmacy, or on the street: some can safely use, while a few cannot. Far more success in resolving society's woes would be gained by focusing law enforcement on the problem: alcohol and other drug *addicts*. It is the *person* who needs consequences for misbehaviors that subject their victims to physical and other abuse, including a form of targeted prohibition in which use by those who violate the rights of others is proscribed.

The trouble is that other than driving under the influence (an offense for which few are apprehended), most addicts do not blatantly violate laws for which they can be prosecuted. Until recently, one could seek damages for intentional infliction of emotional abuse only in conjunction with actual physical harm, even if occurring for decades. While emotional distress may be actionable in cases of sexual harassment, defamation and stalking, obscene or intimidating telephone calls rise at most only to the level of a misdemeanor. Anything less than three incidents of stalking or telephone calls in which the sole intent is to harass cannot be litigated. Emotional abuse resulting from breach of contract and adultery, perhaps the most common violations of trust perpetrated by alcoholics, are not causes of action. Likewise, it is difficult to arraign someone for "borrowing" from family and friends; even written notes of indebtedness can be legally bankrupted. One cannot be incarcerated for acting unethically if such acts are not criminal.

Since few addicts engage in blatantly criminal acts and general prohibition is a proven failure, it is incumbent on close persons to inflict consequences in an uncompromising fashion. The idea that a close person—a codependent—should continue living with a practicing addict is rooted in the idea that use of drugs is no one else's business. However, toes will inevitably be stepped on and boundaries crossed if the user has alcoholism. Therefore, once confirmed, the choice of sobriety or separation needs to be offered. If use results in legally chargeable misbehaviors, the law could proscribe the use of any psychotropic drug (legal or not) by that person. Martin and Charlie Sheen know what a life-saving device such "targeted prohibition" can be.

# 7

# Definitions,
# Descriptions & Phrases

## Myth #96 (in part, "half-truth," but fatally flawed)
## The Myth of the Commonly Accepted
## Definition for Alcoholism

The commonly accepted definition of alcoholism is not only inconsistent with early-stage biochemistry, but also describes mostly latter-stage symptoms. *While experts agree that about 10% of the U.S. population have alcoholism, the definition allows for its identification in far fewer than one out of ten.* And, it does little to shed light on behaviors.[162]

    This is the definition that the most important national organizations in the field of alcoholism (National Council on Alcoholism and Drug Dependence) and medical professionals practicing addiction medicine (American Society of Addiction Medicine) jointly agreed to in 1990, with the author's italics:

**"Alcoholism/Chemical Dependency is a primary, chronic disease with genetic, psychosocial and environmental factors influencing its development and manifestation. The disease is often progressive and fatal, and is characterized by continuous or periodic:**
**1.** *impaired control over drinking/using,*
**2.** *preoccupation with the drug,*

3. *use of alcohol/drug despite adverse consequences and*
4. *distortion in thinking, most notably denial."*

A look at each section will expose the myths supporting this definition and show that it is ineffective in attempting to diagnose early-stage alcoholism.

### "Alcoholism/Chemical Dependency..."
The term "dependency" suggests a physical dependence on the substance, which as seen in the biochemistry may not occur for decades.

### "...a primary, chronic disease with genetic, psychosocial and environmental factors influencing its development and manifestation."
Correct, but with a caveat. It is genetic; some children get it, some don't. It skips around generations, as do many diseases. The virulence of the strain inherited, psychology of the person, circumstances and environment combine to influence the form addiction takes. The definition is flawed, however, in failing to point out that its inception is essentially 100% predetermined in a person who possesses the necessary alcoholic biochemistry and begins using the drug. By neglecting to include the idea that psychological, social and environmental factors cannot change biochemistry, there is an implication that a person with alcoholism, if properly treated, can safely resume use. As previously mentioned, numerous studies purporting to show this have failed when taking into account long-term control over behaviors. Also, the implication that alcoholism originates in one's environment may be the greatest obstacle to overcoming its stigma.

### "The disease is often progressive and fatal..."
While correct, this does not point to the most gruesome reality of alcoholism: that it is extremely damaging and sometimes fatal *to others,* often long before the afflicted succumbs.

### "... characterized by continuous or periodic..."
The periodic heavy drinker is the most difficult to identify as alcoholic, especially in the early stage when months or even

years may elapse between use. Aside from the fact that this type of alcoholic may never be identified, this statement is correct.

However, the observer may never see the drinking even when use is continuous. The early-stage alcoholic doesn't appear inebriated except at very high BALs, while the latter-stage one is expert at hiding both the drug and its use. This explains an observation made by many addiction experts: alcoholism is never found unless suspected. Therefore, for practical purposes this clue has little or no value in helping observers identify alcoholism.

Note that the four criteria below include an "and" between items three and four, not an "or." This suggests that all four are necessary for a diagnosis of alcoholism.

**"[...characterized by continuous or periodic]** *impaired control over drinking/using..."*
This is the key part of the myth. How did the person with alcoholism get to the point at which he has lost control? As previously described, it can take decades of heavy use for the biochemistry to change. *Loss of control occurs only in latter stage alcoholism,* or by using a drug far more physically addictive than alcohol. Those in the early stage often go for weeks, months or years without drinking, or doing so in moderation much of the time. The poly-drug addict often loses control early on, but the progression into latter-stage addiction at a chronologically young age makes her easier to diagnose. Furthermore, most outsiders (and often, even close persons) are not in a position to observe loss of control over use: it is too often hidden.

The constant craving for the drug as represented in the public's psyche and in movies such as "Lost Weekend" does not occur in the early stage. **Loss of control over use is but a** *symptom* **of alcoholism. Loss of control over behaviors as a result of use** *is* **alcoholism.**

**"[...characterized by continuous or periodic]** *preoccupation with the drug..."*
Until he needs the drug to normalize, why would there be an obsession? Because he knows how extraordinary and righteous

it makes him feel. However, only he knows this; the *feeling* of godliness that occurs in the early stage is not observable by another person. It is unlikely that others will see behaviors indicating an obsession until the latter stage, when a continuous flow of the drug can be found coursing through his veins.

**"[...characterized by continuous or periodic]** *use of alcohol/drug despite adverse consequences..."*
The expression "alcohol/drug" suggests that alcohol is not a drug. The terminology would be greatly improved by saying, "alcohol/other drug," which makes it clear that alcohol is but one category. "Adverse consequences" are: 1. In the eye of the beholder; 2. Often not suffered in the early stage because (a) the alcoholic is protected from consequences by well-meaning family, friends, fans, constituents and law enforcers and (b) over-achievement often compensates for negative consequences; 3. Rarely connected to use by the afflicted because of euphoric recall (viewing words and actions in a self-favoring light). Therefore, "adverse consequences" may not be a useful indicator of alcoholism, especially in the early stage.

**"[...characterized by continuous or periodic]** *distortion in thinking, most notably denial."*
As previously described, alcoholism causes distortions in perception and memory, the most notable of which is euphoric recall. Since this makes the person with early-stage alcoholism believe that he can do no wrong, the drug and biochemistry cannot be the source of problems in his life or in the lives of those around him. It bears repetition that denial implies a willful attempt to not admit to something and self-favoring distortions of perception and memory leave nothing to admit. As stated at the outset, one cannot be in denial about something that he is incapable of seeing.

**"Alcoholism requires all four of the above criteria continuously or periodically."**
Any of these criteria indicate likely alcoholism. Worse, the first two (impaired control over use and preoccupation with the drug) often occur or become observable only in latter-stage

alcoholism or polydrug addiction. Furthermore, since few observers are privy to *any* of the criteria, they are generally useless in diagnosing drug addiction in *any* stage until the addict's life has fallen apart.

The definition misses the descriptor that the early-stage biochemistry predicts: loss of control over *behaviors* and, in particular, destructive conduct. Since these occur near the onset, the behavioral manifestations of addiction need to be an integral part of the description. The following takes these objections into account:

> *Alcoholism is a genetic disorder that causes the afflicted to biochemically process the drug alcohol in such a way as to cause that person to engage in destructive behaviors, at least some of the time.*

The idea that the biochemistry of alcoholics differs from that of non-alcoholics is implicit in this definition. It provides a set of observable symptoms ("destructive behaviors") that are often evident only erratically ("at least some of the time"). This makes it possible to identify those with alcoholism long before obvious late-stage symptoms appear, affording the opportunity for close persons, as well as others acting under the protection or guise of law, to intervene and *prevent* tragedy, rather than react to it.

## Myth #97
## "Alcohol and other drug use is a 'bad habit'."

Tapping one's fingers in a way that annoys others is a bad habit. There is an infinite gap between this and alcoholism.

Such tapping doesn't cause other forms of bad behavior. It doesn't lead to embezzlement, burglary or murder. It doesn't spawn over 300 secondary diseases and disorders or, for that matter, any at all. Nor does it cause one to commit serial adultery or lie and deceive in countless other ways. It doesn't even make a person verbally abusive. *Alcoholism can do all of this.*

In a poor choice of words, news stories inform of well-known actors' and athletes' "bad habits" as "hard to break," or musicians kicking their "heroin habit," or "Hollywood's bad habit." While no one would describe a person with diabetes, cancer or Alzheimer's as having a "bad habit," we use this phrase in depicting the behaviors of celebrities and criminals with alcohol and other-drug addiction. Because dictionaries report common usage, one meaning for "habit" in Webster's is "addiction." However, this use is best relegated to non-chemical compulsions if we are to differentiate between very different concepts. Another definition for "habit" is "something done easily, a practice or custom," giving a sense of something innocuous and voluntary. Terms that compromise the true nature of alcoholism are best shunned if we are to convey accurate meanings. Alcoholism — the biological processing of the drug in a way that causes the afflicted to engage in poor behaviors — is anything but innocuous and voluntary.

## Myth #98
## "'He's an alcoholic!' is an
## appropriate descriptive phrase."

The great linguist S. I. Hayakawa, in *Language in Thought and Action* challenged the idea that words are a result of our thoughts. Using a semantic parable,[163] he described an experiment in relief vs. social insurance in two different towns suffering from high unemployment. In one town, relief was made difficult to obtain, degrading and humiliating, while in the other, social ("unemployment") insurance was viewed as having been earned from work previously performed (the prior work being viewed as a "premium" paid for the insurance). While quarrels, unhappiness, resentment and bitterness toward the recipients were common in the town paying "relief," tranquility increased among the citizenry in the community paying "insurance." While taxpayers in the first town mocked those who ate at the public trough, workers in the other were proud to be able to offer insurance to help those in need. Yet, the stipend paid to every unemployed head of family in each community was identical. Perhaps, Hayakawa suggested, words determine our thoughts and beliefs.

It is significant that Hayakawa's mythical towns have fused in modern-day countries. Unemployment insurance turns into relief, or welfare, only after an extended period, if at all. We view the person drawing "insurance" with far less disdain (if any at all) than we do a person collecting "welfare." Many nearing the end of their unemployment payments do everything possible to avoid accepting welfare. Different words and the way they are used in describing similar acts dramatically color our thoughts and beliefs. Therefore, if a topic is viewed with contempt, the words used to describe might be, at least partially, to blame.

This may be the case for the subject of alcoholism and its identifying label, "alcoholic." A person is called an alcoholic with the same contempt as one is identified as being a leper. A suggestion of alcoholism is usually met with tremendous resistance. "He's too smart," "She's too successful," "She can't be — she's got too much to lose," or a libel suit are a few of the common responses to what seems to many, an accusation.

While we refer to "diabetics" and to a person being "anemic" without disdain, the connotation attached to "alcoholic" has evolved into an extremely negative one. On the other hand, when referring to most other diseased persons, we identify them by saying the person "has" the disease. He has cancer, she has heart disease, or she has pneumonia. Note that a person may be tenderly identified as having epilepsy, but may also be more harshly called an epileptic. Why not convert our words to less accusatory phrases when referring to someone with alcoholism?

We can both educate the non-afflicted *and* more delicately identify the practicing addict with a transformation of vocabulary. We might, for example, suggest that someone who exhibits serially poor conduct is engaging in behaviors "indicative of addiction." Since this disorder causes extreme mood changes, persons exhibiting such mood swings "may have the disease of alcoholism," or simply, "may have alcoholism." This conveys dramatically different inferences than the incriminating-sounding, "he's an alcoholic," or "she's probably an alcoholic." Rather than blaming, we can identify, with the goal of helping others see that a dramatic improvement in behaviors is a virtual certainty if we are right and the person enters a program of recovery.

Self-identification among those with alcoholism may also be an important tool in educating others. One of the many reasons the typical non-afflicted person hasn't a clue about addiction is that so few in recovery readily identify themselves as such. The more often before-and-after comparisons of behaviors are made public, the better educated the non-addicted will become. A recovering person can call attention to any prison, or suggest that the non-afflicted see the Burton-Taylor movie, "Who's Afraid of Virginia Woolf?," for an inside glimpse of his life as a person with active alcoholism.

Yet today, if he self-identifies at all, he does it badly. Those with other diseases never say, "I'm a (name the disease)." "I'm an alcoholic" is a phrase seemingly rooted in the idea that character defects cause alcoholism. This grossly misinforms. "I have alcoholism" is accurate, far more liberating to the afflicted and affords the unaware (almost every non-alcoholic) with a glimmer of understanding. "I have the disease of alcoholism," or even better, "If I drink, there is a great risk that I will act destructively and misbehave in ways I ordinarily wouldn't," are statements that not only provide a concise and accurate explanation, but also open the door to further discussion.

To further clear the air, a modifier for "alcoholism" may be helpful. Few think of someone as having alcoholism if he hasn't already messed up his life on numerous levels. Many believe that someone who is open about his drinking cannot have alcoholism. Yet the process of "hiding" describes a latter-stage symptom. This behavior generally occurs only when others have begun to connect the dots, by which time misbehaviors resulting from addictive drinking have likely caused multiple tragedies. Long before alcoholism becomes obvious, we may hear someone making belittling and disparaging remarks or committing other verbal abuse. We could identify this person as "having behavior patterns indicative (or suggestive) of early-stage alcoholism." The same is true of those exhibiting a "rules don't apply to me" attitude, along with people who use any tactics necessary to win or get their way. Such adolescent-like behaviors are often clues to alcoholism decades before there is a loss of control over drinking.

Words have the ability to shape our attitudes and views. It isn't "just semantics" when we can alter the course of civilization through education. Yet, given the fact that 80 to 90% of incarcerated prisoners have alcoholism and are generally undiagnosed and untreated, we can do exactly that. Extrapolating the idea to those who are less destructive, it is likely that a similar percentage of non-criminally poor conduct or unethical behavior may also be rooted in alcoholism. If true, we could markedly improve our lives and the lives of those close to us through education. The words and phrases we use can play a major part in this process.

# Myth #99
## "He's a 'problem drinker,' not an alcoholic."

In their classic work, *Under the Influence*, James R. Milam and Katherine Ketcham state, "Simply because a man argues with his wife, stomps out of the house, and gets drunk at the corner tavern does not mean that he is an alcoholic. Marital problems and job difficulties are not sufficient by themselves to indicate alcoholism."[164] While these authors refer to this as "problem drinking," another authority, Father Joseph C. Martin, plainly states that *"an alcoholic is a person whose drinking causes problems."*[165] Milam and Ketcham imply that "marital problems and job difficulties" may be less serious than those symptomatic of alcoholism, while Father Martin would likely disagree. Yet the former admit, "in the early stages, alcoholic drinking can easily be confused with normal or problem drinking behavior."[1656]But can it? Is early stage alcoholism truly different from problem drinking, or is problem drinking really early- or middle-stage alcoholism? And, is it ever "normal" to engage in repeated poor conduct that can be linked to drinking?

131

Support for the idea that "problem drinking" is a form of early-stage alcoholism can be found in the observation that erratically bad behaviors associated with drinking eventually worsen in almost every instance. Although sometimes taking decades, long-term observations and interviews with recovering alcoholics provide support for this hypothesis. Most "problem drinkers" eventually descend into latter-stage alcoholism or "stop" drinking. The idea that latter-stage alcoholics pass through earlier stages in which symptoms such as "marital problems and job difficulties" occur is an observable fact.

Biochemistry also supports the idea that such difficulties are symptomatic of early-stage alcoholism. Recall that a build-up of poison on the brain results in distortions of perception, leading to impaired judgment, manifesting in observably destructive behaviors. These vary tremendously from addict to addict, perhaps because the degree to which the poison accumulates may vary. When different upbringings, environment, circumstances and personalities are added to the mix, it shouldn't be surprising that there are as many different manifestations of alcoholism as there are alcoholics. Some are far more destructive than others. In addition, those who stick only to alcohol often progress very slowly in their disease, because all the neurotransmitters are affected but none are specifically targeted. Decades can elapse before alcoholics become obvious, when the brain's ability to produce its own neurotransmitters shuts down. This is very different from other drugs such as heroin, cocaine and almost every pharmaceutical, which target specific neurotransmitters and, therefore, diminish the brain's ability to produce them relatively quickly.

Milam and Ketcham argue that "Problem drinking ...appears to be caused by psychological, emotional, or social problems, while alcoholic drinking is caused by hereditary factors."[167] Yet, when those who appear to be problem drinkers stop drinking, the psychological, emotional and social problems gradually subside. Therefore, they were alcoholics—just a relatively non-lethal variety. Again, it is not "normal" to engage in repeated poor conduct that can be linked to drinking. If there is such conduct, it's alcoholism.

# Myth #100
## "He's a drug abuser, not an addict."

The term "abuse" suggests voluntary action and behavioral choice. Due to a buildup of acetaldehyde in the brain resulting in damage to the neo-cortex, the person with alcoholism does not have a choice as to his behaviors when affected by the substance. Therefore, the phrase "he's a drug abuser" needs to be banished form the lexicon if we are to better communicate the idea that problem behavior is usually rooted in addiction. If bad behaviors are linked to use, he's an addict.

On the other hand, there are those who "abuse" drugs, getting high for a period of time in their lives, but with no lasting negative effect. Fraternity brothers may get stinking drunk while in college only to later move on, having caused no harm to others. It may be difficult without extended observation to identify which are the budding young alcoholics, but by no means do they make up all the party boys and girls. The term "abuse" is deceptive and inappropriate when applied to alcohol or other drug addicts.

Observers are rightly confused when "abuse" is used to describe behaviors indicative of alcoholism. The psychologists' manual, the *DSM-IV*, gives the following as criteria for "substance abuse," requiring that one or more of these occur within a 12-month period:

1. "Recurrent substance use resulting in a failure to fulfill major role obligations at work, school, or home (e.g., repeated absences or poor work performance related to substance use...neglect of children or household)"

**Note that at best this is indicative of middle-stage addiction.**

2. "Recurrent substance use in situations in which it is physically hazardous (e.g., driving an automobile or operatinga machine when impaired by substance use)"

**This almost always begins occurring in
early-stage alcoholism and continues throughout
the drinking and using career.**

3. "Recurrent substance-related legal problems (e.g., arrests for substance-related disorderly conduct)"

**It is amazing that the *DSM-IV* could consider such poor behaviors indicative of "abuse" and not addiction.**

4. "Continued substance use despite having persistent or recurrent social or interpersonal problems caused or exacerbated by the effects of the substance (e.g., arguments with spouse about consequences of intoxication, physical fights)"

**It should be apparent that the *DSM-IV* is referring to full-blown addiction as "abuse."**

What else could they possibly add when the condition that presumably follows substance abuse, "Substance Dependence," is defined? The *DSM-IV* says any three or more of the following occurring within 12 months indicates such a condition:
1. Increased tolerance, requiring more of the substance to become intoxicated
2. Withdrawal, resulting in significant distress or impairment in terms of functioning
3. The substance is taken in larger amounts or over a longer period than intended
4. There are unsuccessful efforts to cut back the use
5. Much time is devoted to obtaining the substance or recover from its effects
6. Important activities are curtailed or given up due to use
7. The use continues despite connecting the dots between use and physical or psychological problems[168]

**It may be obvious that any *one* of these is indicative of middle- or latter-stage addiction.**

The use of these definitions carries enormous weight in the inability of physicians to identify alcoholism. Researchers in a study led by Michigan State University in Kalamazoo set out to determine the rate of "harmful" alcohol use in a primary care population. The team screened 300 adults in a hospital-based, outpatient clinic. While nearly half of the sample had one or more symptoms of such use, only 18% met the *DSM-IV* criteria for alcohol abuse or dependence. Further, only a fraction of these, 17% (or barely over three per cent of the total sample) had been previously treated for alcoholism.[169]

If there is "abuse" there is likely alcoholism. We wait for the medical professional to diagnose it as such only at the risk of multiple tragedies occurring.

## Myth #101
### "Three drinks? He must be an alcoholic!"

Even non-alcoholics can have several drinks over the course of an evening. However, our focus should be on the behaviors. While the absence of poor behaviors over the course of several drinking episodes is not proof of non-alcoholism, if there is serious misconduct during *any* drinking episode, alcoholism should be suspected. However, this is not likely to occur until the drinker's BAL reaches a level far higher than would result from a mere three drinks. If misbehaviors are observed in someone consuming only a few drinks over two or three hours, we should take a closer look. There may be hidden alcohol or other, less observable drugs in the system.

## Myth #102
### "Heroin is more addictive than alcohol."

As mentioned under Myth #11, "Drugs are inherently addictive; every user is a potential addict," even hard drugs require more use than most think necessary before physical addiction occurs. However, the predisposed become mentally addicted to alcohol due to the inherited biochemistry from the glow felt during the first build-up of acetaldehyde. According to almost every recovering alcoholic with more than a few years' sobriety, this usually begins during the first drinking episode. Since these are typically the people who experiment with other drugs, it only *seems* that such drugs are more addicting: to an addict, a drug is a drug, and he is already addicted.

On the other hand, many people using cocaine and heroin recreationally (rare though they may be), as well as legal "hard drugs" such as Oxycontin and Vicodin for pain control, never become addicted. Over 90% of the soldiers using heroin in Viet Nam returned to the U.S. and stopped their use cold turkey. The vast majority of Vicodin users can't wait to get off the drug. Similarly, the vast majority of those who try alcohol *never* become addicted. Yet, the few who do almost always look back when sober and realize they used addictively—and in fact, were addicted—at first use.

## Myth #103 (a "half-truth")
## "He died of an accidental overdose."

It takes a large quantity or variety of medications in the system to die from an overdose. The use of this term is often a euphemism for the truth: he died of alcoholism.

There have been innumerable such accounts in the media. One of the most tragic was the headline reporting the death of movie producer Don Simpson: "Report Says Producer Died of Accidental Overdose." Yet drugs found in Simpson's system included cocaine, along with the prescription drugs Unisom, Atarax/Vistaril, Librium, Valium, Compazine, Xanax, Desyrel and Tigan.[170] Therefore, Simpson died of alcohol and other drug addiction, which is the phrase that best communicates the truth about addiction. The descriptor "accidental" is misleading, since the root cause of death goes unidentified.

## Myth #104 (a "half-truth")
## "He died from injuries sustained from an accident."

It is likely that half of "accidental" deaths are a result of alcoholism. We do not communicate the pervasiveness of addiction by blaming deaths on symptoms. The underlying cause of death when a participant to the incident is under the influence is usually addiction. Therefore, he died from his diseased state, not because of injuries from an accident.

The well-known on-road alcohol-related fatality figure of 40% (about 16,000 out of 40,000 deaths per year) could be low. In fatal accidents, only 75% of drivers are tested for alcohol and none for other drugs. Yet, the National Highway Traffic Safety Administration, in its Field Validation Study of the Drug Recognition Expert program, found that less than four per cent of the suspects who had used other psychoactive drugs had a BAL of .10 per cent or greater.[171] In other words, among suspects using drugs other than alcohol, over 96% were found not legally drunk. Some DREs believe that for every three or four drivers under the influence of alcohol, at least one more is under the influence of other drugs with little or no alcohol in the system. Considering the fact that drugs "potentiate" each other, resulting in a far more powerful punch than any one drug provides by itself (i.e., relatively little of each drug, when combined, does the trick), the fatalities resulting from DUI may be substantially higher than suspected. It would not be surprising if they are closer to the 60% of drivers that the NHTSA study found under the influence when objects or other vehicles were "almost struck."

We find similar numbers in non-vehicular incidents. As previously mentioned (Myth #77), alcohol is estimated to be the cause of 70% of deaths from drowning, 90% of fatalities from fire and about 40% of all industrial fatalities (a statistic remarkably similar to driving casualties).

## Myth #105
## "The cause of death was cancer, heart disease, liver disease, complications from pneumonia, etc."

Indeed, death may have been directly attributable to one of these diseases. However, alcoholism causes or exacerbates 350 secondary diseases and disorders. Therefore, the underlying cause of death is often alcoholism.

We have long cleansed ourselves of human failings so as not to lay blame, cause embarrassment or make someone appear "bad" in the eyes of others. One example of this was a kind of syphilis from which few were reported to have died even though many had long suffered. John Gaunt, who compiled births and deaths in 17th century London, concluded that "most of the deaths from ulcers and sores [of which there were many] were in fact caused by venereal disease, the recorded diagnoses [death from other causes] serving as euphemisms." Death from syphilis was reserved for "hated persons, and such, whose very Noses were eaten of..."[172]

Alcoholism, like syphilis hundreds of years ago, is too-often hidden in the dark recesses of family histories. We hide the cause of death under the technically correct immediate cause, which when viewed from the larger picture, is false.

The stigma of alcoholism resulting in few actually "dying" of the disease at least partially explains the fact that so few understand it. If people die of everything but alcoholism, why should we bother to learn more about it? As a result, as James Graham points out, "alcoholism is probably the most under-studied of all complex subjects."[173] In addition, it's the most under-researched of all major diseases: for every dollar spent each on research for cancer, heart disease and many others, pennies are spent on alcoholism. And yet, it does more peripheral damage than all others combined and, perhaps, more direct damage than any other single cause.

# Myth #106
## "The addict is in denial."

Because of the self-favoring light in which the addict views all of his behaviors, he cannot be in denial. The addict is, instead, incapable of seeing his own problem. This erroneous and misleading phrase is key to propagating the idea that the addict knows better. He does not, nor can he.

# Myth #107
## "The codependent is in denial."

The codependent, or close person, cannot be in denial about something that has never been properly explained and about which few have ever been educated. Addiction needs to be described as a biochemical disorder that causes destructive behaviors, which are often masked by charm. Some may choose to take the bad behaviors along with the charm. While this may indicate low self-esteem in the non-addict, who sits like the proverbial frog in a pot of water brought slowly to a boil, it is not denial.

# Myth #108
## "There must be something wrong with a person who repeatedly falls in love with alcoholics."

As mentioned, addicts are often the most charming people on the planet. Who would not fall in love with the blind Lt. Colonel Frank Slade, portrayed by Al Pacino in the movie "Scent of a Woman," as he sweeps a beautiful young lady onto the dance floor and teaches her the tango?

Further, addicts are adept at spotting easy targets. Those who have grown up with an addict parent are accustomed to volatile behaviors. While they may or may not be comfortable around those exhibiting such conduct, they are often unaware of what is abnormal or unhealthy. When they become involved with such addicts, especially those in the "functional" stage prevailing during much of the drinking career, they just figure it's normal. Seeing the fundamentally good person underneath, they figure that the occasional bizarre behaviors must be tolerated to benefit from the good ones. There is nothing wrong with such people; they just don't know any better. They've never been taught to associate the drinking and using with misbehaviors, especially since the person can be every bit as good or bad while under the influence as when not.

# 8

# Doctors, Alcoholics Anonymous & Treatment

### Myth #109
### "12-Step Programs are religious cults."

As author James Graham pointed out, because alcoholism causes ego-inflation, ego-deflation is essential to recovery. The reason 12-Step Programs work is because steps one through eleven help deflate the alcoholic ego. If this encourages religion, so be it. However, you don't have to believe in God (as many know Him) to belong to AA, or for the Program to work. All that is necessary is acceptance of a power higher than oneself. The alcoholics' belief that he is God or god-like must be shattered for recovery to occur.

There are many agnostics and even a few atheists in AA. One agnostic, who is a believer in the 12-Step Program, is actor John Laroquette. With the help of AA he has remained sober since the early 1980s.

### Myth #110 (a "half-truth")
### "The alcoholic should remain anonymous."

As mentioned, the alcoholic must have his ego deflated for

recovery to occur. The act of announcing to the public that he is in recovery is a potentially ego-inflating device. "Look at me, I have overcome alcoholism," may quickly be followed by relapse. Therefore, he must remain anonymous.

Or so it would seem. Since early-recovery is tentative, unnecessary risks that may promote a relapse are not worth taking. However, this danger dissipates over time. Anonymity is one of the key reasons why the public is ignorant about cause and effect in regard to alcoholism and destructive behaviors. At some point, the benefits of educating the public about the effects of alcoholism may outweigh the risk of relapse. Education includes identifying people who we would never imagine are recovering alcoholics. It is illuminating when an alcoholic in recovery points to the nearest street thug or white-collar criminal and bluntly states, "there, but for the grace of God, go I." The uninitiated is unaware of the millions of recovering alcoholics whose lives—and behaviors—were turned around in sobriety.

Even those who know of such a case often think it's an aberration. They frequently don't grasp the idea that in real sobriety *all* alcoholics undergo a radical personality change when compared to the active alcoholic: the Mr. Hyde the drug had turned them into.

On the other hand, there could be a boon to an early-recovery alcoholic announcing his disease for a very different reason. He could say to close others, "If you see me become destructive, do not believe my denials that I am again using. If I am destructive, I *must* be using. Do not give me money, do not stay with me, do not hire me or believe anything I say. I am probably lying, cheating, stealing and manipulating with some regularity. Offering me uncompromising tough love is by far the best chance to instill in me a desire to become and stay sober." However, since he is extremely unlikely to make such an announcement, others close to him should.

# Myth #111 (a "half-truth")
## "Attending Al-Anon will help you better deal with alcoholism."

Al-Anon is a program for codependents, those romantically, familially or professionally involved with alcoholics. While its message emphasizing caring for oneself is an essential one, it's not where we learn about alcoholism. Until this disease is understood, there is a lingering doubt in our minds that we are doing the right thing by imposing uncompromising tough love on the addicts in our lives. Sitting in on Alcoholics Anonymous meetings is often needed to understand addiction well enough to remove that doubt, helping us to properly deal with alcoholics.

# Myth #112
## "Non-alcoholics are control freaks."

Non-alcoholics often react to the loss of control close addicts have over their own behaviors and lives by attempting to control everything else. They may try to micromanage in a futile effort to get the addict back in line. This reaction does not indicate a truly controlling attitude. Some are controlling in the absence of addiction, but many are not.

The sanctimonious attitude of some who refer to non-addicts as control freaks serves only to take the focus off the truly controlling people—those having a need to wield power over others in an effort to inflate their egos. This psychological need rooted in differential brain chemistry makes addicts the truly great control freaks.

# Myth #113
## "Addicts have to do it for themselves."

This refers to the idea that the need to get clean and sober must come from within. The media perpetuate this myth. In one story, former meth users claim "there was nothing family or friends could have done—compassion, tough love or anything in between—to get them off their drug. They needed to decide on their own." Yet, in the next paragraph, we are informed it took a third arrest and a friend killed before one addict went into treatment.[174] Close analysis usually confirms that few, if any, addicts enter recovery without being dealt consequences that are either tragic or in the nature of uncompromising tough love, such as threat or actual loss of job, security, privilege or family. This clearly comes from outside.

As we have seen, friends, family, employers and law enforcers can coerce abstinence. Many in recovery report that sobriety grew out of this. While they may have *stayed* sober for themselves, it often began with coercion: they stopped using because of pain from appropriate consequences inflicted by others.

## Myth #114 (a "half-truth")
## "The alcoholic needs treatment."

And so he does. More important however, codependents— those in a position to protect the addict from the logical outcomes of misbehaviors—need to be educated about addiction. They must understand it well enough to make enabling—the process of protecting the addict from consequences—something in which they will never again engage.

Treatment often fails because close persons are not convinced that addictive use is at the root of the problem, which makes them willing to continue to put up with poor behaviors. Yet, the odds of permanent sobriety are greatly reduced if there is even one close enabler left in the addict's life. Educating— treating—the codependent is essential to reducing the enabling. The probabilities of long-term sobriety are greatly increased when the addict knows that his misbehaviors will no longer be tolerated.

# Myth #115
## "The family is as sick
## — or sicker — than the alcoholic."

While they need as much help, they are not sicker. Their reactions are normal and, even, predictable.

Non-addicts are sometimes asked, "What was wrong with *you*? Why are you so attracted to alcoholics?" Growing up with an alcoholic parent accustoms one to at least occasionally bizarre or destructive behaviors. This is particularly true when the parents are relatively functional or their parents' friends are alcoholics. Courting an early-stage addict, then, is comfortable because it's a known entity: it's just like home. In addition, the addict knows who the "mark" is. Since his sick ego needs to wield power, he will avoid situations in which such control is unlikely. The attraction, then, is mutual, increasing the odds of such a match.

Since alcoholism is a progressive disease that takes many years to run its course, the non-addict codependent, in many cases raised in an alcoholic home, can be subjected to continuing dysfunction for decades. As George E. Vaillant put it, "outside of residence in a concentration camp, there are very few sustained human experiences that make one the recipient of as much sadism as does being a close family member of an alcoholic."[175] No wonder the family may appear as sick (or even sicker), in terms of observable behaviors, than the addict. In some cases, a spouse may be tentatively identified as a likely alcoholic when, in fact, the other spouse has the disease.

Yet, while the codependent may be sick, he does not suffer brain damage that makes learning new ways, ideas and productive habits impossible. Armed with ideas such as those presented here, he can recover from decades of sick behavior relatively quickly. Because the practicing addict suffers such damage, longer time frames are usually required for full recovery.

# Myth #116
## "Only a medical doctor can diagnose alcoholism."

Any early- to middle-stage alcoholic can appear normal during repeated doctor's visits, making it impossible to spot the disease. Further, few medical doctors are trained to detect alcoholism even when informed about behaviors. Many medical personnel continue to believe that circumstances and environment cause addiction, so are unlikely to identify it in those in having good families and doing well at school or work. Privacy issues make information sharing at best difficult, decreasing the likelihood of even the aware doctor identifying the problem. Since the addict often behaves in public, the best observer is the person privy to events occurring behind closed doors. Many authorities have said that anyone can learn to identify alcoholics; no medical degree is required. Even though they have not explained precisely how to do so, they are right.

# Myth #117
## "Doctors and therapists understand alcoholism."

If they truly understood alcohol and other drug addiction, Dr. Gary Losse's career would have ended far sooner than it did. Losse was among an elite group of surgeons upon whom top professional athletes depend for their health and livelihoods. Despite the fact that suspected "abuse" of prescription painkillers was an open secret for many years, he was the San Diego Chargers' team doctor, performing surgery on its players from 1984 to 1998. Worse, not only did Losse's colleagues fail to intervene; they even prescribed the painkillers for him.

If doctors were to grasp the idea that alcoholism is the root cause of the majority of human misbehaviors, they would stop enabling, intervene and impose consequences at the earliest opportunity. Testifying for plaintiff Dan Berglund, chief investigator for the San Diego County District Attorney's Office, who filed a lawsuit against Losse in 2001, one of Losse's nurses said that by early 1997 his "behavior was becoming increasingly abusive and aggressive," which she recognized as a subtle sign of drug "abuse." Despite the fact that the Medical Board of California estimates that 18% of all doctors "will have substance abuse in their lifetimes," and some estimate that narcotic addiction is 30 times greater among physicians than in the general population, the Medical Board took no action. (They fined Losse $750 in July, 2000 for an unrelated infraction.) Yet, according to court documents, the Chargers were concerned enough about his rumored drug use to ask him to step down in 1998.[176] Yet the odds are, addictive use began decades earlier.

Losse's is not an isolated case. As director of the Talbott Recovery Center in Atlanta, Georgia, Dr. Douglas Talbott has treated over 4,000 addicted doctors and estimates that up to 19% of all doctors are addicts. Unfortunately, the treated are only a fraction of the afflicted; most are never offered a choice of sobriety or loss of license. The fact that appropriate consequences are infrequently prescribed for other doctors suggests that they must not understand the fundamental idea of addiction: that unpredictable and erratically bad behaviors will eventually result, causing unnecessary tragedy for patients.

# Myth #118
## "Doctors and therapists have the tools to diagnose alcoholism."

Most medical professionals are untrained in diagnosing alcoholism. Medical doctors are required to take 24 classroom hours in addiction, largely so they know how to treat an addict in withdrawal. Unless they become addiction specialists, they are taught little or nothing about identifying addiction among patients. Countless recovering alcoholics report well-intentioned doctors prescribing psychoactive drugs, which they used to further their addiction.

Rather than learning that addiction *causes* behavioral disorders, most therapists are taught that addiction *is* a behavioral problem. If it is the latter, the cause(s) of the addictive use must be uncovered for recovery to occur. Because of this assumption, therapists treat symptoms, to no one's benefit.

The failure of two therapists to identify addiction in my fiancée over a decade ago led to the discoveries I have shared. Not once during two years of joint counseling did the therapists suggest the possibility that addiction might explain her increasingly bizarre and destructive behaviors. Yet, she had relapsed into addictive drinking early in the relationship, slowly progressing to prescription pharmaceuticals and culminating in the use of crack cocaine. I have learned first-hand how little most professionals understand about addiction. It is my sincere hope that exploding the myths — particularly, the myth of the definition of alcoholism — will improve the methods by which both professionals and lay persons identify and treat alcoholism — and remove the fear from making that call.

# Appendix I
## Myths by Chapter

### Chapter 1
### Alcoholism Made Simple:
### the Brain, the Biological Process & Inheritance

Myth #1 "Brain damage occurs only in obvious alcoholics."

Myth #2 "The average age at which one becomes an alcoholic is 40."

Myth #3 "Alcoholism is a spiritual disease."

Myth #4 "You can choose not to be an alcoholic."

Myth #5 "The addict is in denial."

Myth #6 "With a Blood Alcohol Level between .10 and .24 per cent, even an alcoholic would appear inebriated."

Myth #7 "Two or three drinks per hour are needed to maintain a given Blood Alcohol Level."

Myth #8 "Three drinks will make anyone legally intoxicated."

Myth #9 (a "half-truth") "He has a hangover because he drank too much last night."

Myth #10 "Light-to-moderate users of alcohol account for most of the lost-work days because they make up most of the work force."

Myth #11 "Drugs are inherently addictive; every user is a potential addict."

Myth #12 "But she's only on Xanax. This shouldn't be a problem; after all, it's only available by prescription."

Myth #13 "I don't use drugs. I only drink."

Myth #14 "Use of so-called 'hard' drugs causes far more destructive behaviors than does alcohol."

Myth #15 "Drugs create addicts by transforming their brains."
Myth #16 "Every drinker is a potential drunkard."
Myth #17 (a "half-truth") "He drinks to escape."
Myth #18 "She drinks because she's unhappy."
Myth #19 "Some drink excessively to compensate for their shyness."
Myth #20 "Excessive drinking can make up for a lack of self-esteem."
Myth #21 "I didn't experience any significant withdrawal symptoms when I quit drinking. Therefore, I can't possibly be an alcoholic."
Myth #22 "Because the gene for alcoholism has never been located, there is no proof that alcoholism is a disease."
Myth #23 (a "half-truth") "Smoking is more dangerous than drinking alcohol."
Myth #24 "He really knows better. He knows what he did and knows he is at fault."
Myth #25 (a "half-truth") "O.J. knows what he did."

# Chapter 2
## Environment, Circumstances, Personality & Gender
Myth #26 "Alcoholism is both genetic and environmental."
Myth #27 "Proper parenting and involvement will prevent alcoholism."
Myth #28 "If he'd had a better upbringing, he wouldn't be an alcoholic."
Myth #29 "Since 60% of children of alcoholics do not develop alcoholism, we can conclude that the disease is not genetically-determined."
Myth #30 "Poor upbringing, environment, circumstances or a combination of these cause alcoholism."
Myth #31 "She was a victim of incest, beatings, or other child-abuse; no wonder she's an alcoholic."
Myth #32 "The stresses of the job and other life problems made her turn to the bottle."
Myth #33 (a "half-truth") "The younger a person begins drinking, the more likely alcoholism is to develop."

Myth #34 "We can teach kids not to use drugs."
Myth #35 "We can prevent use through education, thereby decreasing the number of addicts."
Myth #36 "Since advertising alcohol increases use, it should be banned!"
Myth #37 "Some Personality Types are more likely to be alcoholics."
Myth #38 "A larger percentage of men are alcoholics."

## Chapter 3
## Control over Use

Myth #39 (a "half-truth") "Alcoholics can learn to control their drinking."
Myth #40 (a "half-truth") "I can control my drinking; therefore, she should be able to do so."
Myth #41 "He can't control his drinking."
Myth #42 "Alcoholics lack willpower."
Myth #43 "He never looks drunk—so he can't be an alcoholic!"
Myth #44 "I never see her gulp, so she can't be an alcoholic."
Myth #45 "He drinks by himself, so he must be an alcoholic."
Myth #46 "One who drinks every day, or a lot, must be an alcoholic!"
Myth #47 (a "half-truth") "The trouble is, some people drink too much."

## Chapter 4
## Beauty, Brains & Success

Myth #48 "He can't be an alcoholic—he's getting straight A's and, besides, he's too young."
Myth #49 "She's too successful to be an alcoholic."
Myth #50 "She's too smart to be an alcoholic."
Myth #51 "He's too charming to be an alcoholic!"
Myth #52 "One who never misses a day of work and is rarely late couldn't be an alcoholic."
Myth #53 "He can't be an alcoholic because I've never seen him with red eyes."
Myth #54 "She can't be an alcoholic—look at what great shape

she's in."
Myth #55 "Someone who has everything, including great looks, couldn't possibly be an alcoholic."
Myth #56 "If a person at the top of his profession or social sphere were an alcoholic, the public would know!"
Myth #57 "A person at the top of her profession or social sphere is not likely to remain an alcoholic for very long, because her money will save her. After all, she has access to the best medical care that money can buy."
Myth #58 "He can be reasoned with; after all, he's an intelligent human being."
Myth #59 "Psychological problems stemming from being the child of an alcoholic best explain adolescent-like behaviors in highly intelligent and successful people."

# Chapter 5
# Abuse & Dysfunction

Myth #60 "Most misbehaviors can't be attributed to alcoholism. Those who engage in such behaviors are usually fundamentally bad people and not alcoholic."
Myth #61 "Being a great liar doesn't make a person an alcoholic."
Myth #62 "She just has a insatiable need to win."
Myth #63 "His real personality comes out when he drinks."
Myth #64 "Personality disorders are more common than alcoholism," or a variation, "He's no alcoholic-he's just crazy!"
Myth #65 "He's no alcoholic; he's just a racist."
Myth #66 "He's probably just a harmless 'big talker'."
Myth #67 "Some just lack impulse control."
Myth #68 "The behaviors will improve with anger management counseling."
Myth #69 (a "half-truth") "Power and control are classic signs of a batterer."
Myth #70 (a "half-truth") "He's abusive and probably an alcoholic."
Myth #71 (a "half-truth") "She has low self-esteem; that doesn't make her an alcoholic."

Myth #72 "He got into trouble because of his drinking."
Myth #73 "Most people who engage in destructive behaviors are just bad people."
Myth #74 "I'm a recovering alcoholic and I'm still bad."
Myth #75 "People can change—they just hardly ever do."
Myth #76 "You're either born with a conscience or you're not."
Myth #77 "She's just accident-prone."
Myth #78 "He's just a bad driver, not DUI."
Myth #79 "She's not DUI. She's probably just having a bad day."
Myth #80 "He may be an alcoholic, but he would never risk a child's life by drinking and driving with one."
Myth #81 "She would never hurt anyone."
Myth #82 "He'd never do that!"
Myth #83 "Law enforcers can always be trusted to tell the truth and act appropriately."
Myth #84 "Poverty causes crime."
Myth #85 "In the end, we can negotiate with a madman."

# Chapter 6
## Consequences

Myth #86 "If alcoholism is a disease, the afflicted should not be held responsible for behaviors."
Myth #87 "Friends don't let friends plead guilty."
Myth #88 "If she's an alcoholic, she would have lost her job."
Myth #89 (a "half-truth") "He can't keep drinking—it'll kill him, and that would be tragic."
Myth #90 "We have to wait for her to hit rock-bottom."
Myth #91 "The fact that millions overcome addiction on their own is evidence that alcoholism is not biological and genetic, since they just 'decide' to give it up for no apparent reason."
Myth #92 "The fact that she voluntarily went into a facility for rehabilitation is an act of courage."
Myth #93 "When stopped for a traffic violation, most of those driving under the influence are arrested."
Myth #94 "We shouldn't concentrate on DUIs when there are so many worse crimes committed."
Myth #95 (a "half-truth") "Drug use is a victimless crime."

# Chapter 7
## Definitions, Descriptions & Phrases
Myth #96 (in part, "half-truth," but fatally flawed) The Myth
of the Commonly Accepted Definition for Alcoholism
Myth #97 "Alcohol and other drug use is a 'bad habit'."
Myth #98 "'He's an alcoholic!' is an appropriate descriptive
phrase."
Myth #99 "He's a 'problem drinker,' not an alcoholic."
Myth #100 "He's a drug abuser, not an addict."
Myth #101 "Three drinks? He must be an alcoholic!"
Myth #102 "Heroin is more addictive than alcohol."
Myth #103 (a "half-truth") "He died of an accidental overdose."
Myth #104 (a "half-truth") "He died from injuries sustained
from an accident."
Myth #105 "The cause of death was cancer, heart disease,
liver disease, complications from pneumonia, etc."
Myth #106 "The addict is in denial."
Myth #107 "The codependent is in denial."
Myth #108 "There must be something wrong with a person
who repeatedly falls in love with alcoholics."

# Chapter 8
## Doctors, Alcoholics Anonymous & Treatment
Myth #109 "12-Step Programs are religious cults."
Myth #110 (a "half-truth") "The alcoholic should remain
anonymous."
Myth #111 (a "half-truth") "Attending Al-Anon will help you
better deal with alcoholism."
Myth #112 "Non-alcoholics are control freaks."
Myth #113 "Addicts have to do it for themselves."
Myth #114 (a "half-truth") "The alcoholic needs treatment."
Myth #115 "The family is as sick —or sicker—than the alcoholic."
Myth #116 "Only a medical doctor can diagnose alcoholism."
Myth #117 "Doctors and therapists understand alcoholism."
Myth #118 "Doctors and therapists have the tools to diagnose
alcoholism."

# Endnotes

1. James E. Royce and David Scratchly, *Alcoholism and Other Drug Problems*, New York: The Free Press, 1996, p. 133.

2. George E. Vaillant, *The Natural History of Alcoholism Revisited*, Cambridge, MA: Harvard University Press, 1995, p. 21.

3. Donald W. Goodwin, M.D., *Is Alcoholism Hereditary?* New York: Ballantine, 1988, pp. 102-103, found that children of alcoholics raised by non-alcoholics are four times as likely to develop alcoholism as are children of non-alcoholics, yet show no difference in the incidence of psychopathological behavior, depression, anxiety neurosis and personality disturbances.

4. The Wall Street Journal, "No Easy Fixes," op-ed piece, March 7, 2001.

5. The Los Angeles Daily News, "'An angry young man': Motive of teen suspect elusive," Todd S. Purdum of The New York Times, March 7, 2001.

6. Vernon E. Johnson, *I'll Quit Tomorrow*, San Francisco, CA: Harper and Row, 1980, p. 43-45.

7. C.A. Pristach, C.M. Smith and R.B. Whitney, "Alcohol withdrawal syndromes-prediction from detailed medical and drinking histories," Drug Alcohol Dependence, April 11, 1983; 11(2): 177-99.

8. Richard Rovere, *Senator Joe McCarthy*, 1960: Methuen & Co., Ltd., quoted in James Graham, *The Secret History of Alcoholism: The Story of Famous Alcoholics and Their Destructive Behavior*, Rockport, MA: Element Books, 1996, p.21.

9. www.about.com web site: www.alcoholism.about.com/library/weekly/aa000613a.htm, June 18, 2002.

10. Jeffrey Wiese, MD and Michael Shlipak, MD, MPH, "The Alcohol Hangover," Annals of Internal Medicine, June 6, 2000 Vol. 132 issue 11, pp. 897-902 and March 20, 2001 Vol. 134, issue 6, p. 534.

11. James A. Inciardi, *The War on Drugs: Heroin, Cocaine, Crime, and Public Policy*, Mountain View, CA: Mayfield Publishing Company, 1986, pp. 61-62.

12. Newsweek, "I Am Addicted to Prescription Pain Medication," October 20, 2003, p. 49.

13. The Contrarian's View, January 31, 2001, p. 9, citing federal judge John L. Kane.

14. The New York Times, "Daughter of Gov. Bush is Sent to Jail in a Drug Case," Dana Canedy, July 17, 2002.

15. Newsweek, "A 'Very Serious Problem'," February 11, 2002, p. 8.

16. Patty Duke and Kenneth Turan, *Call Me Anna: The Autobiography of Patty Duke*, New York: Bantam Books, 1987, pp. 90-91, 155, 169, 174, 196, 200-201, 203-205, 239 and 310.

17. Prevention File, "Drugs and Violence: What's the Link?" Winter, 2002, pp. 17-19, citing research at the Robert Presley Center for Crime and Justice Studies at the University of California, Riverside, published in the "Annual Review of Sociology."

18. Drug Abuse and Alcoholism Newsletter, "Drugs and Violence," Sidney Cohen, Vista Hill Psychiatric Foundation, April, 1973.

19. Ibid.

20. National Review, "How the Narcs Created Crack," Richard Cowan, December 5, 1986, pp. 30-31, cited in Cato Institute Policy Analysis, "Thinking About Drug Legalization," James Ostrowski, May 25, 1989, p. 50.

21. Ostrowski, Ibid. pp. 20 and 47-48.

22. Parade Magazine, "My Life Changed Forever," Dotson Rader, October 5, 2003, p. 5.

23. Royce and Scratchley, Ibid. p. 132, citing studies by James R. Milam and Rae H. Farmer.

24. Audrey Kishline, *Moderate Drinking: The Moderation Management Guide for People Who Want to Reduce Their Drinking*, New York: Crown Trade Paperbacks, 1994, p. 5; italics in the original.

25. James Graham, Ibid. p. 99.

26. Vaillant, Ibid. pp. 96-97; italics in the original.

27. Donald Goodwin, MD, *Is Alcoholism Hereditary?* New York: Ballantine Books, 1988, pp. 98-115.

28. Lucy Barry Robe, *Co-starring Famous Women and Alcohol: The Dramatic Truth Behind the Tragedies and Triumphs of 200 Celebrities*, Minneapolis, MN: CompCare Publications, 1986, p. 172.

29. Vaillant, Ibid. pp. 104-108.

30. Martha Morrison, *White Rabbit: A Doctor's Story of Her Addiction and Recovery*, New York: Crown Publishers, 1989, p. 10.

31. Associated Press, "RFK's son accused of having affair with teen-age baby sitter," April 26, 1997.

32. The Los Angeles Daily News, "Skakel felt his brother stole his girl, ex-classmate testifies," John Christoffersen, Associated Press, May 18, 2002.

33. The New York Times, "Celebrity's Son: Big Connections And Addictions: Ordeal of Moyers Family Underlies a TV Documentary," by Christopher S. Wren, March 24, 1998.

34. Playboy, "The Demons that Drove Don Simpson," Bernard Weinraub, June, 1996, p. 160.)

35. In his book *Heavy Drinking: The Myth of Alcoholism as a Disease*, Herbert Fingarette argued that, in Dr. Goodwin's studies, since 82% of the adopted-out sons who had a biological alcoholic father were not identified as alcoholics, we cannot conclude there is a disease of genetically determined alcoholism. Berkeley, CA: University of California Press, 1988, pp. 52-53.

36. Graham, Ibid., in a footnote on p. 3.

37. Wendy Maltz, *The Sexual Healing Journey: A Guide for Survivors of Sexual Abuse*, New York: HarperPerennial, 1992, p. 31; italics in the original.

38. The Los Angeles Daily News, "Whitney's guru: Showbiz to blame," March 24, 2004.

39. Johnson, Ibid. p. 2.

40. The Los Angeles Times, "Quitting Is Just the First Step," Lynn Smith, October 1, 2000, citing The Center for Alcohol and Addiction Studies at Brown University in Providence, Rhode Island, as well as other authorities.

41 Dennis P. Rosenbaum and Gordon S. Hanson, "Assessing the Effects of School-Based Drug Education: A Six-Year Multi-Level Analysis of Project D.A.R.E.," Journal of Research in Crime and Delinquency, Vol. 35 No. 4, November, 1998. The authors point out that studies reporting positive results for D.A.R.E. are not longitudinal, which would measure the long-term success rate for the program.

42. The Wall Street Journal, "Drug Czar Says Ad Campaign Has Flopped," Vanessa O'Connell, May 14, 2002.

43. Seattle Post-Intelligencer, "Campus alcohol program 'short on proof': Harvard researcher says method has no positive effect on student drinking," Jake Ellison, July 24, 2003, reporting on a study led by Harvard researcher Henry Wechsler.

44. The Los Angeles Times, "Focus on the Other Costs of Drunk Driving: A federal ad campaign hammers home the legal implications-arrest and loss of license," Sharon Bernstein, July 8, 2003.

45. Royce and Scratchley, Ibid. pp. 31-32.

46. David Keirsey and Marilyn Bates, Please Understand Me: Character & Temperament Types, Del Mar, CA: Prometheus Nemesis Book Company, 1978.

47. Maria Roy, Ed., Battered Women: A Psychosociological Study of Domestic Violence, New York: Van Nostrand, 1977, p. 39.

48. www.vix.com/pub/men/battery/battery.html, November, 1997.

49. Glenn Sacks, "Let's not 'Learn' the Same Lessons From Blake That We Learned From OJ," May 7, 2002, www.GlennSacks.com, citing the U.S. Department of Justice's Special Report-Violence Against Women.

50. Glenn Sacks, Ibid.

51. The Los Angeles Daily News, "Domestic Abuse is Two-Way Street," Norah Vincent, June 26, 2003, who cites Richard Gelles, dean of the University of Pennsylvania School of Social Work and the National Coalition of Anti-Violence Programs.

52. Vaillant, Ibid. p. 301.

53. Vaillant, Ibid. p. 281.

54. M. L. Pendery, I. M. Maltzman and L. J. West, "Controlled Drinking by Alcoholics? New Finding and a Reevaluation of a Major Affirmative Study," Science, 1982, 217:169-175.

55. Vaillant, Ibid. p. 302.

56. John A. Ewing and Beatrice A Rouse, "Failure of an Experimental Treatment Program to Inculcate Controlled Drinking in Alcoholics," British Journal of Addiction, 1976, 71: 123-34.

57. Royce and Scratchley, Ibid. p. 138.

58. Kishline, Ibid.

59. Associated Press, "Moderation Management Debated," Mia Penta, June 27, 2000.

60. "Dateline," NBC News, 30 Rockefeller Center, New York City, NY 10112, August 26, 2997; transcript by Burrelle's Information Services, Box 7, Livingston, NJ 07039, pp. 9-13.

61. Kishline, Ibid. p. 13, citing Society, "Drugs and Free Will," J.A. Schaler, September/October 1991, p. 47.

62. Morrison, Ibid. pp. 24, 34, 53, 79 and 101.

63. Ibid. p. 19-21, 37 and 144.

64. Playboy, "Sinatra and the Dark Side of Camelot: Frank and JFK had a lot in com-

mon: Gangsters, starlets, hookers and unquestioned power," George Jacobs (who worked as Sinatra's valet from 1953 to 1968) and William Stadiem, June 2003.

65. The Los Angeles Daily News, "Sizemore had earlier domestic-abuse run-in," Linda Deutsch, August 8, 2003.

66. USA Weekend, "From rough seas to smooth sailing," Mary Roach with Evelyn Poitevent, November 19-21, 1999, p. 9.

67. Vanity Fair, "Nothing Left to Fear," Carl Bernstein, December, 1999, p. 158.

68. The Los Angeles Daily News, "Stone jailed; no conspiracy cited," June 12, 1999.

69. The Wall Street Journal, "Report Says Producer Died of Accidental Overdose," March 27, 1996.

70. The Los Angeles Daily News, L.A. Life, "Singer for Three Dog Night pens his sobering story," Marilyn Beck and Stacy Jenel Smith, December 4, 1997, p. 2.

71. The New York Times Magazine, "Band on the Couch," Chuck Klosterman, June 20, 2004.

72. Robe, Ibid. pp. 47-48.

73. The Wall Street Journal, "Drink and Grow Rich," Op-ed piece, May 2, 2002.

74. Donald Goodwin, M.D., Alcohol and the Writer, Kansas City: Andrews and McMeel, 1988, cited in Graham, Ibid. p. 8.

75. The Economist, "Hands across a century," August 30, 2003, p. 60.

76. Donald H. Dunn, Ponzi! The Boston Swindler, New York: McGraw-Hill Book Company, 1975, p. vii; italics in the original.

77. Ibid. p. 179.

78. Ibid. p. 128.

79. Ibid. p. 253.

80. Graham, Ibid. p. 108.

81. Robe, Ibid. p. 96; Barbara Rowes, Grace Slick: the Biography, Garden City, NY: Doubleday & Company, Inc., 1980, p. 71.

82. www.katu.com/news/story.asp?ID=46916.

83. The Los Angeles Daily News, "Van Damme cited for drunk driving," September 24, 1999.

84. Ottawa Sun, "Clean break for Jean-Claude," Louis B. Hobson, August 31, 1998.

85. Golf Magazine Online, "Daly to enter Betty Ford Clinic after alcohol relapse," March 30, 1997.

86. American College of Sports Medicine Journal: Medicine and Science in Sports and Exercise, "Alcohol and college athletes," Toben F. Nelson and Henry Weschsler of the Harvard School of Public Health, cited in an Internet post January 21, 2001, Associated Press, "Study: Athletes Drink More Alcohol."

87. The Los Angeles Daily News, "'Charmed' star suspected of DUI," David Greenberg, December 29, 2000.

88. Robe, Ibid. p. 2.

89. Robe, Ibid. pp. 525, 528, 537 and numerous other pages.

90. **Moore:** USA Weekend, "From rough seas to smooth sailing," Ibid.; **Quaid:** Vanity Fair, "Madcap with a Twist," December, 1999, p. 364; **Johnson:** The Los Angeles Times Calendar, "The Life of His Own Party," Paul Brownfield, March 28, 1999, p. 8-9, 84 and 86.

91. The Los Angeles Times, "Herbalife's Supplement Supplier in Failing Health," Jerry Hirsch, October 13, 2000.

92. Newsweek, "Flying a Little Too High: An alert screener keeps impaired pilots on the ground," Arian Campo-Flores, July 15, 2002, p. 25.

93. Benjamin Parsons, *Anti-Bacchus: An Essay on the Crimes, Diseases and Other Evils Connected with the Use of Intoxicating Drinks*, 1840; cited in James R. Milam and Katherine Ketcham, *Under the Influence: A Guide to the Myths and Realities of Alcoholism*, New York: Bantam Books, 1983, p. 81.)

94. Graham, Ibid. p. 107.

95. B. D. Hyman, *My Mothers Keeper: A daughter's candid portrait of her famous mother*, New York: William Morrow and Co., 1985, p. 277; italics in the original.

96. Doug Thorburn, *Drunks, Drugs & Debits: How to Recognize Addicts and Avoid Financial Abuse*, Northridge, CA: Galt Publishing, 2000, pp. 166-170, provides a fascinating and thorough description of these behaviors.)

97. B. D. Hyman, Ibid. p. 269.

98. Royce and Scratchley, Ibid. p. 132.

99. The balance of this section is largely excerpted from Doug Thorburn, *How to Spot Hidden Alcoholics: Using Behavioral Clues to Recognize Addiction in its Early Stages*, Northridge, CA: Galt Publishing, 2004, with permission of the publisher.

100. The role of Psychological Type and Temperament in diagnosing and treating addiction is discussed in Thorburn, *Drunks, Drugs & Debits*, Ibid. pp. 245-272 and 331-338, and in greater detail in Doug Thorburn, *Styles of Alcoholism: The Role of Type and Temperament in Diagnosing and Treating Addiction*, Northridge, CA: Galt Publishing, publication expected in 2005. This is in turn derived partly from David Keirsey and Marilyn Bates, Ibid, and Keirsey's student, Eve Delunas, *Survival Games Personalities Play*, Carmel, CA: SunInk Publications, 1992. *Styles of Alcoholism* links the Survival Games played by different Temperaments to specific Personality Disorders mimicked by addiction.

101. *Diagnostic and Statistical Manual of Mental Disorders, Fourth Edition*, Washington, DC: American Psychiatric Association, 1994. This is known as the "*DSM-IV*."

102. *DSM-IV*, Ibid. pp. 649-650.

103. *The 16th Edition of the Merck Manual*, 1992, p. 1546.

104. Terence Gorski, "The Role of Codependence in Relapse" audio cassette series, Independence, MO: Herald House/Independence Press, 1991.

105. Leonard L. Heston, M.D., and Renate Heston, R.N., *The Medical Casebook of Adolf Hitler*, New York: Stein and Day, 1980.

106. Duke and Turan, Ibid.

107. Anne Wilson Schaef, "Recovering in an Addictive World," audio-tape, 10th Annual "Common Boundary" Conference, Boulder, CO: Sounds True Recordings, 1991.

108. Families of the Mentally Ill Collective, Nona Dearth, Chairman, *Families Helping Families Living With Schizophrenia*, New York: Avon Books, 1987, p. 7.

109. Henry Maudley, M.D., *Responsibility in Mental Disease*, New York: D. Appleton and Company, 1897, pp. 305-306, citing D. Yellowlees, M.D., "Insanity and Intemperance," *British Medical Journal*, October 4th, 1893. Maudley also noted in his discussion of what he termed "the indulgence" in liquor that "Short of the...undeniable ills which it is admitted on all hands to produce, it is at the bottom of manifold mischiefs that are never brought directly home to it." I am not the first to point out the fact that numerous behavioral problems that *should* be linked to

alcoholism are not.

110. *DSM-IV*, Ibid. p. 651.

111. *DSM-IV*, Ibid. p. 661.

112. Success is usually thought of in commerce and is closest to the Guardian in the Keirseyan Temperament paradigm, or SJ in the Myers-Briggs Type Indicator. In the same vein, brilliance is Rational or NT, beauty is Artisan or SP, ideal love is Idealist or NF, while power over people is SP and power over ideas is NT.

113. Royce and Scratchley, Ibid. p. 132.

114. The Los Angeles Times, "Eldridge Cleaver's Last Gift: the Truth," David Horowitz, my copy of article undated.

115. The Wall Street Journal, "Hitler's Heirs: German Skinhead Tells Court, 'I Am a Racist,' As Neo-Nazis Spread," Greg Steinmetz, August 3, 1998.

116. The Los Angeles Daily News, "Killer learned hatred during college years," Bill Dedman, The New York Times, July 6, 1999; www.psychassault.org/manufacture3.html.

117. Abraham H. Maslow, *Motivation and Personality*, New York: Harper and Row, 1970, pp. 43-45.

118. Dan Carter, *The Politics of Rage*, New York: Simon & Schuster, 1995, p. 104.

119. Marshall Frady, *Wallace*, New York: Random House, 1996, p. 81.

120. Playboy, George Jacobs and William Stadiem, Ibid.

121. The Wall Street Journal, "As Nation Wobbles, Venezuelan Leader Tightens His Grip," June 12, 2003 p. 1.

122. Cited by Robe, Ibid. p. 157.

123. National Review, "Bad Attitude," Margaret A. Hagen, July 20, 1998, p. 38, interpreting studies by Neil Jacobson and John Gottman of the University of Washington, in addition to other studies.

124. Maria Roy, Ed., Ibid., p. 39.

125. The Los Angeles Daily News, "We've seen a monster who looks just like us," Joseph Honig, September 22, 2002.

126. The Los Angeles Daily News, "Suspect's ex-girlfriend tells of foul drunk mood," Seth Hettena of the Associated Press, July 11, 2002.

127. *Alcoholics Anonymous: The Story of How Many Thousands of Men and Women Have Recovered from Alcoholism*, New York: Alcoholics Anonymous World Services, Inc., Third Edition, 1976, p. 542.

128. Forbes, "Cerebral Celebrity," January 8, 2001, p. 44, citing bill O'Reilly, *The O'Reilly Factor*, p. 38.

129. Success, "The Good Fight: Defeat Your Enemies - Both Without and Within," February, 1996, p. 102.

130. NCADD Fact Sheet: "Alcohol and Other Drugs in the Workplace," National Council on Alcohol and Drug Dependence, Inc., 12 West 221 Street, New York, NY 10010; National Institute on Drug Abuse, "Research on Drugs and the Workplace," NIDA Capsules, June, 1990; D. Campbell and M. Graham, "Drugs and Alcohol in the Workplace: A Guide for Managers," New York: Facts on File Publications, 1988, p. 9.

131. STAND, Support Training Against Narcotic Dependency, Los Angeles Police Department handout, "Why STAND?"; Thomas E. Backer, Ph.D., "Strategic Planning for Workplace Drug Abuse Programs," National Institute on Drug

Abuse, 1987, p. 4.

132. Robe, Ibid. p. 402, citing a report of the National Council on Alcoholism.

133. B.D. Hyman, Ibid. p. 195.

134. STAND, Ibid.

135. Newsweek, "A 'Very Serious Problem'," February 11, 2002, p. 8.

136. National Highway Traffic Safety Administration, *DWI Detection and Standardized Field Sobriety Testing: Student Manual*, Oklahoma City, OK: U.S. Department of Transportation, October 1995, pp. V-3 through V-8.

137. Doug Thorburn, *Get Out of the Way! How to Identify and Avoid a Driver Under the Influence*, Northridge, CA: Galt Publishing, 2002 provides far greater analysis of this study, as well as logical extrapolations.

138. NASA study, reported in USA Today, June 12, 2000.

139. The Journal of the American Medical Association, "Characteristics of Child Passenger Deaths and Injuries Involving Drinking Drivers," Kyran P. Quinlan, MD, et al, May 3, 2000, 283:2249-2252.

140. ABCNews.com, Melanie Axelrod, June 20, 2000, reporting on a study conducted by the Ford Motor Company and the University of Michigan Transportation Research Institute.

141. Andy Logan, *Against the Evidence: The Becker-Rosenthal Affair*, New York: Avon Books, 1970, cited in Graham, Ibid. pp. 24-26.

142. Logan, Ibid. p. 266.

143. Ibid. p. 372.

144. Ibid. pp. 342-343.

145. Ibid. p. 349.

146. Ibid. p. 370.

147. The Los Angeles Times, "Former LAPD Officer Suspected of Running a Ring of Robbers," Scott Glover and Matt Lait, May 11, 2003.

148. Thorburn, *Drunks, Drugs & Debits*, Ibid. pp. 14-15 and 91-93, supports this case.

149. The Wall Street Journal, "Jurors Examine Costs of Décor Chez Kozlowski," Scott Thurm, December 16, 2003, p. B1.

150. A compelling case for this is made in Thorburn, *Get Out of the Way!*, Ibid.

151. Royce and Scratchley, Ibid. p. 172

152. Parade Magazine, "My Life Changed Forever," Dotson Rader, October 5, 2003, pp. 4-6.

153. Rudolf Dreikurs, M.D., *Children: the Challenge*, New York: The Penguin Group, 1990.

154. People Magazine, "Rock Bottom," March 29, 2004 p. 69.

155. National Enquirer, "Whitney's Family Stages Intervention to Get Her Into Drug Rehab," Patricia Shipp and Robin Mizrahi, March 25, 2004.

156. National Highway Traffic Safety Administration, Ibid. p. 11-4.

157. The Los Angeles Daily News, "Woman arrested after knife attack on man, son," Associated Press, July 6, 2003.

158. National Highway Traffic Safety Administration, Ibid. p. II-4.

159. The number of incidents needed for one arrest divided by the average number of DUIs per year yields these numbers: 500 divided by 80 equals over six; 2000 divided by 80 yields 25. A yearly arrest rate of one for every 123 licensed drivers in the United

States supports this estimate. Since approximately 12 (10% of 123) of those drivers have alcoholism, if each alcoholic was apprehended only once it would take 12 years to arrest them all on charges of DUI.

160. From a conversation November, 2003 with Holly Hopkins Odom, Executive Director, I Saw You Safety & Scholarship Foundation, Inc., 4400 Bayou Boulevard, Suite 12, Pensacola, Florida 32503; www.1866ISawYou.com; 1-866-472-9968.

161. This section is largely excerpted from Thorburn, *How to Spot Hidden Alcoholics*, Ibid. with permission of the publisher.

162. S. I. Hayakawa, *Language in Thought and Action*, New York: Harcourt, Brace and Company, 1949, pp. 2-6.

163. Milam and Ketcham, Ibid. p. 97.

164. Father Joseph C. Martin, *Chalk Talks on Alcohol*, New York: HarperCollins Publishers, 1982, p. 75; italics in the original.

165. Milam and Ketcham, Ibid. p. 97.

166. Milam and Ketcham, Ibid. p. 41.

167. *DSM-IV*, Ibid. p. 181-185.

168. www.pharmiweb.com/News/reuters/19drug04.asp, October 19, 2000, "News From Reuters: Nearly half of primary care patients have symptoms of alcohol problems," citing a report in the September/October, 2000 issue of the Archives of Family Medicine, p. 814-821.

169. The Wall Street Journal, "Report Says Producer Died of Accidental Overdose," March 27, 1996.

170. LAPD Web Site, www.cityofla.org/LAPD/traffic/dre/ drgdrvr.htm: Thomas E. Page, "The Drug Recognition Expert Response to the Drug Impaired Driver," pp. 5-6.

171. Peter L. Bernstein, *Against the Gods: the Remarkable Story of Risk*, New York: John Wiley and Sons, 1996, pp. 80-81; archaic spelling, etc., in the original.

172. Graham, Ibid. p. xiii.

173. The Los Angeles Times, "Highly Addictive Drug Knows No Boundaries," October 12, 2003, p. B15.

174. Vaillant, Ibid. p. 22.

175. The San Diego Union-Tribune, "Surgeon's habit was open secret, records allege: Co-workers saw signs, depositions say, but patients kept in dark," David Hasemyer and David Washburn, March 10, 2002.

# Bibliography

*Alcoholics Anonymous: The Story of How Many Thousands of Men and Women Have Recovered from Alcoholism*, New York: Alcoholics Anonymous World Services, Inc., Third Edition, 1976.

Bernstein, Peter L., *Against the Gods: the Remarkable Story of Risk*, New York: John Wiley and Sons, 1996.

Carter, Dan, *The Politics of Rage*, New York: Simon & Schuster, 1995.

Delunas, Eve, *Survival Games Personalities Play*, Carmel, CA: SunInk Publications, 1992.

*Diagnostic and Statistical Manual of Mental Disorders, Fourth Edition*, Washington, DC: American Psychiatric Association, 1994.

Dreikurs, Rudolf, M.D., *Children: the Challenge*, New York: The Penguin Group, 1990.

Duke, Patty and Turan, Kenneth, *Call Me Anna: The Autobiography of Patty Duke*, New York: Bantam Books, 1987.

Dunn, Donald H., *Ponzi! The Boston Swindler*, New York: McGraw-Hill Book Company, 1975.

Families of the Mentally Ill Collective, Nona Dearth, Chairman, *Families Helping Families Living With Schizophrenia*, New York: Avon Books, 1987.

Frady, Marshall, *Wallace*, New York: Random House, 1996.

Goodwin, Donald, M.D., *Alcohol and the Writer*, Kansas City: Andrews and McMeel, 1988.

Goodwin, Donald, MD, *Is Alcoholism Hereditary?* New York: Ballantine Books, 1988.

Gorski, Terence, "The Role of Codependence in Relapse" audio cassette series, Independence, MO: Herald House/ Independence Press, 1991.

Graham, James, *The Secret History of Alcoholism: The Story of Famous Alcoholics and Their Destructive Behavior*, Rockport, MA: Element Books, 1996.

Hayakawa, S. I., *Language in Thought and Action*, New York: Harcourt, Brace and Company, 1949.

Heston, Leonard L., M.D., and Heston, Renate, R.N., *The Medical Casebook of Adolf Hitler*, New York: Stein and Day, 1980.

Hyman, B. D., *My Mothers Keeper: A daughter's candid portrait of her famous mother*, New York: William Morrow and Co., 1985.

Inciardi, James A., *The War on Drugs: Heroin, Cocaine, Crime, and Public Policy*, Mountain View, CA: Mayfield Publishing Company, 1986.

Johnson, Vernon E., *I'll Quit Tomorrow*, San Francisco, CA: Harper and Row, 1980.

Keirsey, David and Bates, Marilyn, *Please Understand Me: Character & Temperament Types*, Del Mar, CA: Prometheus Nemesis Book Company, 1978.

Kishline, Audrey, *Moderate Drinking: The Moderation Management Guide for People Who Want to Reduce Their Drinking*, New York: Crown Trade Paperbacks, 1994.

Logan, Andy, *Against the Evidence: The Becker-Rosenthal Affair*,

New York: Avon Books, 1970.

Maltz, Wendy, *The Sexual Healing Journey: A Guide for Survivors of Sexual Abuse*, New York: HarperPerennial, 1992.

Martin, Father Joseph C., *Chalk Talks on Alcohol*, New York: HarperCollins Publishers, 1982.

Maslow, Abraham H., *Motivation and Personality*, New York: Harper and Row, 1970.

Maudley, Henry, M.D., *Responsibility in Mental Disease*, New York: D. Appleton and Company, 1897.

Milam, James R. and Ketcham, Katherine, *Under the Influence: A Guide to the Myths and Realities of Alcoholism*, New York: Bantam Books, 1983.

Morrison, Martha, *White Rabbit: A Doctor's Story of Her Addiction and Recovery*, New York: Crown Publishers, 1989.

Robe, Lucy Barry, *Co-starring Famous Women and Alcohol: The Dramatic Truth Behind the Tragedies and Triumphs of 200 Celebrities*, Minneapolis, MN: CompCare Publications, 1986.

*Merck Manual, The 16th Edition of the*, Whitehouse Station, NJ: Merck & Co., 1992.

Rovere, Richard, *Senator Joe McCarthy*, New York: Harcourt, Brace, Jovanovich, 1959.

Rowes, Barbara, *Grace Slick: the Biography*, Garden City, NY: Doubleday & Company, Inc., 1980.

Roy, Maria, Ed., *Battered Women: A Psychosociological Study of Domestic Violence*, New York: Van Nostrand, 1977.

Royce, James E. and Scratchly, David, *Alcoholism and Other Drug Problems*, New York: The Free Press, 1996.

Schaef, Anne Wilson, "Recovering in an Addictive World,"

audio-tape, 10th Annual "Common Boundary" Conference, Boulder, CO: Sounds True Recordings, 1991.

Thorburn, Doug, *Drunks, Drugs & Debits: How to Recognize Addicts and Avoid Financial Abuse*, Northridge, CA: Galt Publishing, 2000.

Thorburn, Doug, *Get Out of the Way! How to Identify and Avoid a Driver Under the Influence*, Northridge, CA: Galt Publishing, 2002.

Thorburn, Doug, *How to Spot Hidden Alcoholics: Using Behavioral Clues to Recognize Addiction in its Early Stages*, Northridge, CA: Galt Publishing, 2004.

Thorburn, Doug, *Styles of Alcoholism: The Role of Type and Temperament in Diagnosing and Treating Addiction*, Northridge, CA: Galt Publishing, in publication 2006.

U.S. Department of Transportation, *DWI Detection and Standardized Field Sobriety Testing: Student Manual*, Oklahoma City, OK: National Highway Traffic Safety Administration, 1995.

Vaillant, George E., *The Natural History of Alcoholism Revisited*, Cambridge, MA: Harvard University Press, 1995.

# Index

## A

AA (see Alcoholics Anonymous)
Abandonment, psychological, 37-38
Abstinence, coercing, 77, 96, 114, 116, 119-120, 144
Abuse, child, 42, 78
Abuse, emotional, 122
Abuse, financial, 31, 66-67, 93-94, 108, 127
Abuse, physical, 24, 32, 42, 52, 73, 78, 93-94, 105
Abuse, verbal, 38, 52, 79, 89, 93, 130
Accident-prone as a clue to alcoholism, 101-102
Accidents, alcohol related, 2, 29, 39, 51-52, 101-102, 120-121, 136-137
Accusations, false, 18, 52, 78-79, 106-107
Acetaldehyde, 8, 12, 26-27, 81, 86, 95, 110, 133, 135
Actors/actresses and alcoholism, 21, 23, 27, 55-56, 62-64, 68-70, 80, 85, 101, 115, 122, 128, 141
Advertising, alcohol, 47-48
Adopted children of alcoholics, 36, 100
Adultery, 74-75, 79, 106, 122
Aerosmith, 64
Al-Anon, 143
Alcohol-income puzzle, 64
Alcoholics Anonymous, 32, 39, 55, 59, 72, 78, 81, 89, 97, 141, 143, 145, 147
Alcoholism, definition of, 123, 148
Alcoholism, history of, 44
Alcoholism, stigma of, 38, 138
Alice in Chains, 64
Allen, Tim, 62
American Society of Addiction Medicine, 123
Ancestry and Alcoholism, 35-36
Anti-Social Personality Disorder, 83-84
Arafat, Yasser, 69
Arrogance as a clue to alcoholism, 71, 87-88, 94
Athletes and alcoholism, 32, 62, 69
Auld, Christopher, 64

**B**
Backstreet Boys, 64
BAL (see Blood Alcohol Level)
Barrett, Syd, 63
Barrymore, Drew, 62
Basal ganglia, 81, 92, 109
Beach Boys, 64
A Beautiful Mind (movie), 85
Becker, Charles, 107
Beethoven, 64
Beiderbecke, Leon "Bix", 64
Belushi, John, 62
Betty Ford Center, 50, 58
Bingeing, 12, 26, 62, 69-70, 85
Biochemistry, 3, 7, 10-11, 24, 26-28, 31, 35-37, 41-42, 47-50, 60, 73, 78, 81-82, 84, 86, 90, 92, 95, 98, 100, 108-109, 117, 120, 123-127, 132-133, 135
Bipolar Disorder, 61, 83-85
Blackouts, 12, 27, 32, 39, 79, 97, 117
Blaylock, Daron Oshay "Mookie", 62
Bleeth, Yasmine, 69
Blige, Mary J., 64
Blood Alcohol Level, 8, 13-18, 26, 50, 55-57, 59-60, 68-69, 100, 119-120, 125, 135, 137
Bohler, Tamara K., 120
Borderline Personality Disorder, 83, 86
Brain Damage, 7-9, 30, 60, 78, 95, 98, 117
Broderick, Juanita, 73
Buckey family, 78
Bundy, Ted, 10, 67, 77-78
Burton, Richard, 55-56, 62
Bush, Sr., George, 63
Bush, George W., 38, 63, 74
Bush, Jeb, 21, 38, 101
Bush, Noelle, 21, 101
Butler, Yancy, 70

**C**
Campbell, Glenn, 64
Charm, alcoholic, 10, 65-67, 139
Chavez, Hugo, 91
Chemical dependency experts, 2, 14, 108, 115
Cleaver, Eldridge, 88

Hangovers, 17-18
Harding, Tanya, 69
Harlow, Jean, 70
Harrell, Wilson, 99
Harris, Eric, 10, 77
Hartman, Brynn, 105
Hartman, Phil, 105
Harvard's School of Public Health, 69
Hayakawa, S. I., 128
Hayward, Susan, 70
Hemingway, Ernest, 65
Hermany, Sven, 88
Hetfield, James, 64
Hitler, Adolf, 84, 90-91, 109
Holiday, Billie, 64
Hopkins, Anthony, 56
Houston, Whitney, 43
Howe, Steve, 69
Hughes, Mark, 70, 72
Hussein, Saddam, 109
Hyman, B. D., 80, 101

**I**
I Saw You Safety & Scholarship Foundation, Inc., 120-121
Intervention, 4, 47, 112, 115, 118
Invincibility, sense of, 28, 74, 82, 97, 99
Isoquinolines, 8
Iverson, Sherrice, 100

**J**
Jackson, Michael, 105
Jackson, Samuel L., 63
Jefferson Airplane, 67
Johnson, Andrew, 63
Johnson, Don, 70
Johnson, Judy, 79
Johnson, Lyndon, 63
Johnson, Vernon E., 43
Jones, Brian, 63
Jones, Jim, 90
Jonestown, Guyana, 90
Jong Il, Kim, 109

Sade, 64
Sartre, Jean-Paul, 65
Scent of a Woman (movie), 139
Schaef, Anne Wilson, 85
Schaler, Jeffrey, 60
Schizophrenia, 83, 85
Scott, George C., 62
Self-esteem, 28-29, 49, 94, 139
Semmelweis, Ignas, 30
Sex Pistols, 64
Shatner, Nerine, 70
Sheen, Charlie, 27, 70, 115-116, 122
Sheen, Martin, 115-116, 122
Simpson, Don, 40, 63, 136
Simpson, Nicole Brown, 32
Simpson, O.J., 32
Sinatra, Frank, 62
Sizemore, Tom, 62
Skakel, Michael, 39
Slade, Lt. Colonel Frank, 139
Slater, Christian, 62
Slick, Grace, 67
Smith, Benjamin, 89
Smoking, 10, 31, 60, 104
Sobell Study, 53-54
Sociopathic Personality Disorder, 50, 84
Sorkin, Aaron, 63
Spector, Phil, 64
Spencer, Herbert, 65, 75
Spencer, John, 63
Staley, Layne, 64
Stalin, Joseph, 26, 109
Steinbeck, John, 65
Stone Temple Pilots, 64
Stone, Oliver, 63
Strawberry, Darryl, 62, 69
Strohmeyer, Jeremy, 77, 100
Sutherland, Edwin, 109

**T**
Tapia, Johnny, 62
Taylor, Elizabeth, 62, 69

Temperaments, four basic human, 36, 49-50, 87, 115
Three Dog Night, 63
Tower, John, 63
Turner, Ted, 63, 113
Tyler, Steven, 64

**V**
Vaillant, George E., 54, 145
van Dam, Danielle, 95
Van Damme, Jean-Claude, 69
Van Dyke, Dick, 62
Vicious, Sid, 64
Vincent, Norah, 52

**W**
Wallace, George, 90
Watson, George, 58
Webber, Chris, 62
Weiland, Scott, 64
Westerfield, David, 95-96
Whitman, Charles, 106
Who, the, 63, 145
Who's Afraid of Virginia Woolf? (movie), 130
Wiley, Kathleen, 74
Williams, Charles Andrew, 10
Williams, Hank, 64
Williams, Paul, 64
Williams, Robin, 62
Willpower, 56-57, 60
Wilson, Brian, 64
Wood, Natalie, 70
Writers and alcoholism, 65, 75, 111

# About the Author

Doug Thorburn is one of the world's foremost experts in identifying alcoholism based on behavior patterns. He has spoken to and provided continuing education for professional organizations, including the California Association for Alcohol and Drug Educators (CAADE), the California Association of Alcohol and Drug Abuse Counselors (CAADAC), and the California Association of Drinking Driver Treatment Programs (CADDTP).

In addition, Doug has authored three books prior to **Alcoholism Myths and Realities:** *Removing the Stigma of Society's Most Destructive Disease* — **How to Spot Hidden Alcoholics:** *Using Behavioral Clues to Recognize Addiction in its Early Stages* (2004), **Get Out of the Way!** *How to Identify and Avoid a Driver Under the Influence* (2002) and **Drunks, Drugs & Debits:** *How to Recognize Addicts and Avoid Financial Abuse* (2000). He is currently writing **Styles of Alcoholism:** *Using Psychological Type and Personality Disorders to Identify and Treat Addiction* (in publication 2006).

Doug is also the president and founder of the PrevenTragedy Foundation, a non-profit organization dedicated to educating the public on the importance of early identification of alcoholism and how to identify this disease *before* tragedy strikes.

# Other Books by Doug Thorburn

## *How to Spot Hidden Alcoholics*

An essential addiction resource, *How to Spot Hidden Alcoholics* demonstrates how subtle, seemingly innocuous behaviors are often early indicators of alcoholism that occur long before the alcoholic has lost control over drinking.

"Essential for anyone struggling to make sense of the destructive or bizarre behaviors found in others."

Claudia Black, author, *It Will Never Happen to Me!*

"An innovative and enlightening examination that eloquently describes...how to identify [alcoholism] in its early stages based on behaviors...Every counselor, psychologist, physician and interventionist should read this book."

Wallace D. Winters, MD, Ph.D., Emeritus Professor Pharmacology, Towxicology, Anaesthesiology, University of California, Davis, School of Medicine; retired, US FDA Medical Officer, Pacific Region

"An invaluable resource for treatment professionals."

Joan Harter, Past-President, California Association for Alcohol and Drug Educators (CAADE); Professor, Alcohol/Drug Studies, San Bernardino Valley College

"...should be required reading..."

Katherine Ketcham, co-author, *Under the Influence*, *Beyond the Influence* and *Teens Under the Influence*

"Explaining countless tragic events that are otherwise nonsensical, Doug Thorburn makes an incontrovertible case that no dysfunction, including poverty, illiteracy and racism, causes more damage to society than alcohol and other drug addiction. A must read for every social commentator and anyone else who cares about the human condition."

Shawn Steel, former Chairperson, California Republican Party

# Order Form

Fax Orders: 818.363.3111          Phone Orders: 800.482.9424
www.PrevenTragedy.com
Galt Publishing; P.O. Box 7777; Northridge, CA 91327

___ copies of *Alcoholism Myths and Realities* @$14.95 each   $_____
___ copies of *How to Spot Hidden Alcoholics* @ $14.95 each   $_____
___ copies of *Get Out of the Way!* @ $12.95 each   $_____
___ copies of *Drunks, Drugs & Debits* @ $19.95 each   $_____

Sales Tax: 8.25% for California residents   $_____
We pay shipping
                              Total Investment   $_____

I wish to pay by:
_____ Check (enclosed)
_____ Visa          _____ Mastercard          _____ Discover
Card Number: _____ _____ _____ _____   Exp. __ /__
Name on Card: _____
Signature (required): _____

Deliver to: Name _____
            Address _____
            City _____ State ___ Zip Code _____

Telephone Number : _____
Email Address (for updates and to receive the FREE online
Thorburn Addiction Report): _____

Please send additional information on:
            ___ Other books and tapes by Doug Thorburn
            ___ Quantity prices on books
            ___ Speaking & Seminars